NATURAL SUPERFOODS

150 NUTRIENT-PACKED RECIPES FOR COMPLETE HEALTH, VITALITY AND HEALING

SUSANNAH BLAKE

NOURISH
EAT WELL, LIVE WELL

Natural Superfoods

Susannah Blake

First published in the United Kingdom and Ireland in 2015
by Nourish, an imprint of Watkins Media Limited
19 Cecil Court
London WC2N 4HE

enquiries@nourishbooks.com

Recipes taken from *The 5 A-Day Menu Planner*,
first published in 2008 by Duncan Baird Publishers.

Managing Editor: Sarah Epton
Editors: Alison Bolus and Paula Bartimeus
Managing Designer: Clare Thorpe
Commissioned Photography: Simon Smith and Toby Scott
Food Stylist: Mari Mererid Williams
Prop Stylist: Helen Trent

A CIP record for this book is available from the British Library

ISBN: 978-1-84899-228-3

10 9 8 7 6 5 4 3 2 1

Typeset in Avant Garde Gothic
Colour reproduction by Scanhouse, Malaysia
Printed in China

Publisher's Note: While every care has been taken in
compiling the recipes for this book, Watkins Media
Limited, or any other persons who have been involved in
working on this publication, cannot accept responsibility
for any errors or omissions, inadvertent or not, that may
be found in the recipes or text, nor for any problems that
may arise as a result of preparing one of these recipes.
If you are pregnant or breastfeeding or have any special
dietary requirements or medical conditions, it is advisable
to consult a medical professional before following any of
the recipes contained in this book.

Notes on the recipes
Unless otherwise stated:
Use medium eggs
Use fresh herbs
Do not mix metric and imperial measurements
1 tsp = 5ml   1 tbsp = 15ml   1 cup = 250ml

nourishbooks.com

CONTENTS

INTRODUCTION

FOOD IS YOUR FRIEND

In a culture where we are bombarded with messages about food – eat this; don't eat that; don't eat too much; don't eat too little – it's sometimes hard to remember two simple facts: Food is your friend. And food is super!

So-called "superfoods" are those that contain an amazing range of compounds beneficial to good health. There's lots of general advice such as "eat more fruit and veg" but let's take a more targeted look at how those foods with super, health-promoting properties can affect specific areas of the body and your health.

The vast majority of natural, unprocessed foods are packed with nutrients and health-giving compounds that are just waiting to make your body a little bit stronger and work just a little bit better. Your body needs these natural foods and the nutrients that they contain to perform to its very best. So what counts as natural and unprocessed? As a general rule, fruits, vegetables, nuts, grains and pulses, fish, shellfish, meat, eggs and milk are just the basic ingredients for an everyday healthy diet. They all contain a wealth of super-nutrients to help you to be a better you, and to enable your body to work just that little bit harder and more efficiently.

For many of us, it's not just a matter of boosting our immune system or making sure our digestive system is working as well as it can, there is also the spectre of those "big" illnesses such as cancer, a stroke, heart disease and high blood pressure. The good news is that it is widely believed that upping your fruit and vegetable intake can reduce the risk of heart disease, stroke and cancer by up to 20 per cent. In fact, eating more fruit and vegetables is considered to be the second most important tactic for cancer-prevention after cutting down on cigarettes. As for heart disease, it's been found that each increase of just 1 portion of fruit and vegetables a day can lower the risk of coronary heart disease by 4 per cent and that of a stroke by 6 per cent.

Eating more fruit and vegetables can also help to lower blood pressure; bananas and dates are a good source of potassium, which helps to control blood pressure – and there are numerous other health benefits too, including preventing cataract development, improving bowel function thanks to increased fibre content, reducing the symptoms of asthma and helping to manage diabetes.

Packed with vitamins and minerals and health-boosting nutrients, fruit and vegetables contain unique plant components called phytochemicals, such as flavonoids and carotenoids, which help to protect and supercharge the body. Many phytochemicals contain antioxidant properties that help to neutralize free radicals (unstable molecules that damage cells) in the body and also slow down the ageing process. Fresh fruit and vegetables are full of live enzymes that aid the digestive process, and because they are alkaline-forming they help to detoxify the system and alkalize the blood, and help your body produce and maintain a healthy pH balance. A lack of alkaline-forming foods in the diet can lead to all kinds of problems, including muscle aches, arthritis and gout.

Eating plenty of fruits and vegetables can help you to achieve your dietary goals, including increasing fibre and fluid intake, reducing fat intake and helping to keep your weight under control.

A HEALTHY BALANCE

When it comes to food and health, the key word every time is "balance". That means plenty of carbohydrates for energy, loads of fruit and vegetables, enough protein and dairy foods, and just the right amount of the right kinds of fats. Use the handy diagram on page 8 for a quick check on the kind of proportions we're talking about.

USING THIS BOOK

The book covers all your superfood basics, helping you to make the right diet choices every time, even providing you with a selection of targeted menu ideas to get you thinking the superfood way. The recipe collection makes the most of the natural foods at our disposal. Each recipe packs a total health punch by working in as many health-boosting ingredients as possible, providing you with essential variety, balance, flavour and – of course – a wealth of superfoods.

To make the recipes even easier to use for the health-conscious among us, a simple symbol key tells you at a glance how many portions of fruits and vegetables you're going to get in each serving. Every recipe contains at least 2 portions per individual serving, and many contain 3 or 4.

 = 1 full portion

There need be no more tricky calculations over what you should eat for dinner to make up for a skipped breakfast and hurried lunch. Just pick 1, 2 or 3 of these superfood-rich recipes a day and in no time you'll find you're eating at least 5 a day with ease and feeling fantastic.

Note that fat, which is important in a healthy diet, needs to be of the right type and in the correct quantities. Saturated fat can raise cholesterol levels in the blood, which can increase the risk of heart disease. Unsaturated fat is healthier and lowers cholesterol. Try to cut down on foods that are high in saturated fats, such as meat pies and sausages, butter, cheese and cream, and instead choose foods containing unsaturated fats, such as unrefined vegetable oils, oily fish, avocados, nuts and seeds. Also cut down on salt, which can lead to a rise in blood pressure, in turn increasing the risk of heart disease and stroke. Salt is hidden in so many of the everyday foods we eat, such as bread, cereals, sauces, soups and ready meals. Aim to cut down to no more than 6g/¼oz salt a day. (Children need to eat less.)

Another key to good health is water. It's not a superfood but it is essential for a healthy body. Aim to drink at least 8 glasses (2 litres/ 70fl oz/8 cups) of water or other fluids every day. In warm weather, or when you are active, you'll need to drink more than this. Avoid sugary or fizzy drinks, which can contribute to tooth decay, and caffeinated drinks such as coffee and tea, which can contribute to fluid loss.

VARIETY, VARIETY, VARIETY

Once you've got the idea of balance cracked, remember the mantra: variety, variety, variety. The best way to make the most of all those lovely ingredients that are so readily available to us is to eat the widest variety of foods possible. Yes, blueberries are jam-packed with powerful health-promoting antioxidants, but carrots are packed with beta-carotene and strawberries are full of vitamin C. Each food contains its own unique blend of nutrients and health-boosting compounds, so the best way to take advantage of this natural goodness is to eat as wide a mix of foods as possible. This way, you'll be providing your body with as much of the good stuff as you can.

FAT & SUGAR

MEAT & FISH

FRUIT & VEGETABLES

MILK & DAIRY

BREAD, CEREALS & POTATOES

There's such a bounty of choice available in even the smallest stores and supermarkets these days that selecting a variety of foods is never going to be a problem. And the great thing about keeping your diet varied is that it's never going to get boring. Choosing lots of different fruits, vegetables and other ingredients is going to expand not only the health potential of the food you eat but also the appeal of your diet. Who wants to eat the same old dishes day in, day out when – with a little imagination (or at least the help of the recipes in this book!) – you can create a wealth of simple, filling, delicious dishes. Everyone loves to go back to their old favourites, but by eating the superfood way, you've got the chance to discover a range of new favourites as well.

GETTING YOUR 5-A-DAY THE SUPERFOOD WAY

Everyone knows that you're supposed to eat at least 5 portions of fruit and veg a day for good health, but this is also a great way to make the most of everyday superfoods and the nutrients they contain. Fruit and veg are a veritable treasure trove of these nutrients and health-boosting compounds so it makes sense to consume as many of them as you can. Aim to eat at least 5 a day and you'll be well on your way to feeling fantastic.

With busy lives and hectic schedules, demanding jobs and even more demanding family lives, it can sometimes be hard to include those all-important portions. The good news is that this book is designed to help you eat at least 5 a day without you even noticing! You can still grab a piece of toast for breakfast and a sandwich at lunchtime – but add a juice or smoothie at breakfast and make it one of our delicious sandwiches or wraps for lunch and you'll find you've eaten 5 portions of fruit and vegetables before you even start thinking about what to eat for your evening meal. Clearly marked with the number of portions of fruit and vegetables that each recipe provides – every recipe contains at least 2 portions of fruit and veg. (Check out pages 16–19 for more tips on using the recipes and boosting the superfoods in your diet.)

WHAT IS A PORTION?

As a general rule, a single portion for an adult is equivalent to:

- 80g/2¾oz fresh, frozen or canned fruit or· vegetables
- 150ml/5fl oz/scant ⅔ cup fruit or vegetable juice (not from concentrate)
- 1 heaped tablespoon dried fruit
- 3 heaped tablespoons beans or pulses
- 1 dessert bowl of salad.

See the table on the next page to get a clearer idea of exactly what these mean.

QUICK PORTION CHECKER

This quick reference chart shows you how much of each fruit and vegetable you need to eat to consume an 80g/2¾oz portion. All quantities given are approximate and assume a medium fruit or vegetable, unless otherwise stated. If a fruit or vegetable needs to be peeled, cored, deseeded and/or pitted before use, do this before you measure it. You can also use this chart to help you do your shopping. For example, if a recipe calls for 320g/11oz (4 portions) of carrots, you'll need about 4 medium carrots. Portion sizes for young children can be smaller at 60–70g/2¼–2½oz.

Please note, though, that some foods count as only 1 portion in a day, no matter how much you drink or how many you eat (see the note on page 12). However, every gram of fresh, frozen or canned fruit and vegetable counts – so dive in and start adding up those portions!

FRUIT OR VEGETABLE	QUANTITY	FRUIT OR VEGETABLE	QUANTITY
FRESH FRUIT		Passion fruit	5–6
Apples	1	Peaches	1
Apricots	3	Pears	1
Bananas	1	Pineapples	1 large slice
Blackberries	1 handful	Plums	2
Blueberries	1 handful	Raspberries	1 handful
Cherries	1 handful	Satsumas	2
Clementines	2	Sharon fruit	1
Currants, black, red and white	1 handful	Strawberries	about 7
Figs	2	Tangerines	2 small
Grapefruit	½	Watermelon	3cm/1¼in slice
Grapes	1 handful	**CANNED FRUIT**	
Kiwi fruit	1 large	Apple purée	2 heaped tbsp
Kumquats	6–8	Apricot halves	6
Lychees	6	Cherries	3 heaped tbsp (about 11)
Mandarins	1	Fruit salad	3 heaped tbsp
Mangoes	⅓	Grapefruit segments	3 heaped tbsp (about 8 segments)
Melons	5cm/2in slice		
Nectarines	1	Mandarin segments	3 heaped tbsp
Oranges	1	Peach halves	2
Papayas	½	Peach slices	7

QUICK PORTION CHECKER

Pineapple chunks	12	Beansprouts	2 handfuls	
Pineapple rings	2	Beetroot, cooked	3 baby or 7 slices	
Prunes	6	Broccoli	2 spears/florets	
Raspberries	20	Brussels sprouts	8	
Rhubarb	5 chunks	Cabbage	⅙ small cabbage	
Strawberries	9	Carrots	1	

DRIED FRUIT

		Cauliflower	8 florets	
Apple rings	4	Celery	2–3 sticks	
Apricots	3	Chinese leaves	⅕ head	
Banana chips	1 handful	Courgettes	½ large	
Cherries	1 heaped tbsp	Cucumber	5cm/2in piece	
Currants	1 heaped tbsp	Kale, chopped	4 heaped tbsp	
Dates	3	Karela	½	
Figs	2	Leeks	1, white portion only	
Peaches	2 halves	Lettuce	1 dessert bowl	
Pears	2 halves	Mangetouts	1 handful	
Pineapple	1 heaped tbsp	Mushrooms, button	14	
Prunes	3	Mushrooms, sliced	3 handfuls	
Raisins	1 heaped tbsp	Okra	16	
Sultanas	1 heaped tbsp	Onions	½	

JUICES

		Parsnips	1 large	
Fruit juices	150ml/5fl oz/scant ⅔ cup	Peas	3 heaped tbsp	
Fruit smoothies	150ml/5fl oz/scant ⅔ cup	Peppers	½	
Vegetable juices	150ml/5fl oz/scant ⅔ cup	Radishes	10	

FRESH VEGETABLES

		Spinach	1 dessert bowl	
Artichokes (globe)	2	Spring greens	4 heaped tbsp	
Asparagus	5 spears	Spring onions	8	
Aubergines	⅓	Sugarsnap peas	1 handful	
Avocados	½	Sweetcorn, baby	6	
Beans, broad	1 handful	Sweetcorn on the cob	1	
Beans, French, sliced	1 handful	Tomatoes	1	
Beans, runner, sliced	1 handful	Tomatoes, cherry	7	

QUICK PORTION CHECKER

CANNED/BOTTLED VEGETABLES & PULSES

Ackee	3 heaped tbsp	Beans, runner, sliced	4 heaped tbsp
Artichoke hearts	2	Carrots, sliced	3 heaped tbsp
Asparagus	7 spears	Chickpeas	3 heaped tbsp
Beans, black-eyed	3 heaped tbsp	Peas	3 heaped tbsp
Beans, broad	3 heaped tbsp	Pigeon peas	3 heaped tbsp
Beans, butter	3 heaped tbsp	Spinach, chopped	3 heaped tbsp
Beans, cannellini	3 heaped tbsp	Sweetcorn	3 heaped tbsp
Beans, flageolet	3 heaped tbsp	Tomato purée	1 heaped tbsp
Beans, French	4 heaped tbsp	Tomatoes, plum	2
Beans, kidney	3 heaped tbsp	Tomatoes, sundried in oil	4 pieces

A NOTE ON QUALITY & QUANTITY

While beans and pulses do count, they can be considered as only 1 portion each day, no matter how much you eat of them. This is because, although they are a great source of protein and contain valuable fibre and many nutrients, they don't offer the same combination of vitamins, minerals and other health-giving compounds as fruit and vegetables.

Dried fruit also counts as only 1 portion, no matter how much you eat of it. The reason for this is that dried fruit doesn't contain the same quantity of nutrients as fresh, frozen or canned. It also provides a concentrated source of calories and sugars, and so eating large amounts of dried fruit could lead to weight gain and tooth decay.

Fruit and vegetable juices are a delicious way of getting lots of vitamins, but can be counted only once a day. They contain none of the fibre that is present in the whole fruit or vegetable and the process of juicing breaks down the cells, releasing "free sugars", which cause tooth decay, especially when drunk between meals. You tend to consume more of the juice than you would of the whole fruit so you risk having too many calories.

Potatoes and other tubers, such as sweet potatoes, yams, taro, cassava or manioc, do not count as a portion, even though they are vegetables. This is because they have a high starch content, and so are regarded as forming the starchy carbohydrate part of a meal, in the same way that pasta and rice do.

EAT A RAINBOW

When it comes to fruit and vegetables, follow this simple message – "eat a rainbow" – every day to ensure you make the most of the wealth of health-boosting nutrients that they contain. Fruit and vegetables are not only rich in vitamins, minerals and other nutrients, they're also packed with substances known as phytochemicals, which are believed to help protect against illnesses such as stroke, heart disease, some cancers, osteoporosis and urinary tract infections, and protect against the effects of ageing.

Many phytochemicals are related to plant pigments – the substances that give fruits and vegetables their colour. So a simple way to make sure you're getting lots of different phytochemicals is to eat lots of different-coloured fruit and vegetables, rather than just large quantities of, say, apples or carrots. And eating lots of different-coloured fruit and vegetables will ensure you're getting a good range of vitamins and minerals too.

WHITE

Onions, garlic, leeks and the other members of the onion family, such as shallots, spring onions and chives (though chives aren't white, of course!), all possess sulphur-containing compounds, which are thought to reduce the risk of cancer, lower cholesterol and blood pressure, and prevent the blood from becoming sticky, which can lead to strokes. These foods also contain antimicrobial properties that aid the body's ability to fight infection.

Soya beans and soya products such as tofu and soya milk are rich in phytochemicals called isoflavones. These are precursors to active plant oestrogens, which help to regulate female hormone levels and may reduce the risk of certain cancers, such as breast and prostate cancer. They have also been found to lower cholesterol, ease the symptoms of menopause and regulate bone renewal. Soya intake is suggested as one of the reasons why Japanese women have a lower prevalence of bone fractures even though they consume less calcium than Western women.

ORANGE & YELLOW

Carrots, squash, yellow and orange peppers, mangoes and apricots are just a few of the yellow and orange vegetables and fruits that are rich in carotenoids. About 600 different carotenoids have now been identified, all of which possess powerful antioxidant activity, protecting tissues from cancer-forming agents. The body is able to convert some of these carotenoids into vitamin A, which is required for efficient immune function, normal growth and development of the embryo and foetus, and good skin health.

The carotenoid lutein, which gives sweetcorn its yellow colour, is credited with promoting eye health. Research has shown that consuming foods high in lutein can help to reduce the risk of macular degeneration and cataracts.

RED

Tomatoes, pink grapefruit, watermelon, papaya and pink guava are all rich in the red pigment lycopene, another member of the carotenoid family, which is thought to help fight against heart disease and some cancers. Cooking and processing, such as canning, breaks down the lycopene, making it easier for the body to absorb, so, unlike many nutrients, cooking and processing actually makes lycopene more readily available, making canned and puréed tomatoes a great choice. Another beneficial red pigment is betacyanin, which is found in beetroot. Besides being an antioxidant, it is believed to help detoxify the liver.

PURPLE & BLUE

Dark blue and purple fruit and vegetables such as blueberries, plums, black grapes, cherries, raspberries and red cabbage are a great source of anthocyanins. These phytochemicals are powerful antioxidants that are believed to help protect the body against ageing. They also help to promote collagen

EVERY COLOUR EVERY DAY

See how simple it is to eat a colour from every group throughout the day. When you plan your meals, think ahead and pick a different-coloured fruit or vegetable from the one(s) in your previous meal and you'll soon see how easy it is to keep your diet delicious and varied.

- Drink a glass of orange juice when you get out of bed.
- Scatter a handful of blueberries over your breakfast cereal.
- Eat a bowl of creamy onion soup for lunch.
- Serve a spinach and tomato salad with your dinner.

ALTERNATIVELY

- Drink a purple mixed berry smoothie for breakfast.
- Snack on a few dried apricots mid-morning.
- Eat a bowl of pasta with tomato sauce for lunch.
- Serve grilled chicken with stir-fried broccoli and spring onions for dinner.

synthesis (collagen is an elastic-like material responsible for the scaffolding of body tissues) and strengthen blood capillaries. In addition, they have anti-inflammatory properties.

GREEN

The green pigment found in many leafy green vegetables is due to a substance called chlorophyll. It has a stimulating effect on red blood cell production and binds to cancer-forming agents in the gut, preventing them from being absorbed. Green vegetables such as broccoli, cabbage, Brussels sprouts, kale and watercress are rich in the phytochemicals known as glucosinolates, which include indoles and isothiocyanates. These compounds are thought to play a crucial role in helping to protect against cancer.

PACKING IN THOSE SUPERFOODS

Probably the easiest way to make the most of superfoods in your diet is to be realistic about yourself and your lifestyle. Don't obsess about over-loading at every meal – instead, just try to be flexible and enjoy these delicious ingredients in an easy way that fits in with your hectic schedule. If you're meeting friends for dinner, don't panic about what to choose – just enjoy yourself and choose a health-boosting breakfast, such as Tropical Fruit Smoothie (see page 42), and lunch, such as Creamy Carrot, Leek & Tomato Soup (see page 68), instead.

It would be great if everyone could stop for a leisurely, relaxing, healthy lunch every day, but sometimes that's just not an option. Again, don't worry – just make sure you choose a superfood-rich breakfast such as Creamy Fresh Fruit Muesli (see page 46) and dinner such as Chicken Fajitas with Avocado Salsa (see page 112) instead. With the great choice of recipes in this book and the handy fruit and veg portion symbol key, we've done all the hard work for you. Now you just need to do the shopping!

GOOD SHOPPING SENSE

Always shop wisely. Organic vegetables and fruit grown without the use of chemicals and fertilizers are the best choice, but non-organically grown produce is good too – just be sure to scrub it really well or peel off the skin before you eat or cook it so you're not eating any chemicals along with the nutrients.

If you try to buy seasonally, when fruit and vegetables are in abundance, you'll find that they're not only at their freshest but also cheaper, because they're widely available. They taste better, too. Tomatoes ripened in hot summer sunshine until they're sweet, rich and juicy are so much better than the pale, watery specimens you can buy all year round. Vegetables such as asparagus and sweetcorn taste infinitely better and pack a heftier nutrient-punch when they're freshly picked, so you're better off buying locally and in season. When you buy out of season, the produce has often been picked days before, wrapped in cling film, flown for thousands of kilometres and then transferred from one depot to another before arriving on the supermarket shelves and finally your plate – so, not surprisingly, the food just doesn't taste as good and the nutrients have already started to diminish.

However, it's good to remember that it's not just fresh foods that can contribute to your superfood diet. Canned and frozen fruit and vegetables can make a great contribution too, and are an invaluable standby when life is busy and you need to rustle up an instant meal from the store cupboard. Always make sure you've got some in the kitchen for instant meals and desserts. Frozen and canned vegetables have been prepared before processing, which cuts down on your own preparation time. This is great news for busy people trying to boost the healthy ingredients in their diet. All you have to do is throw a portion or two of beans, peppers, peas or corn into a sauce or dish – and it's absolutely no extra effort at all. Fruit canned in juice makes a healthy dessert and frozen berries are great for tossing into fruit compotes, crumbles, ice creams and smoothies.

It's also important to remember that frozen fruit and vegetables can sometimes be more nutritious than fresh. When they're frozen immediately after picking, the nutrients are preserved perfectly. By contrast, the nutrients in fresh fruit and vegetables continue to deteriorate in the time between picking and cooking – so the frozen peas you eat for your dinner may well be packed with more nutrients than the "fresh" ones you podded yourself but were picked some days ago.

Juices and dried fruit are another store cupboard standby that can make a valuable contribution to your 5-a-day quota. Keep a carton or more of juice in the fridge so you can have a glass every day, and keep a selection of dried fruits such as sultanas, apricots, figs, prunes and goji berries in the kitchen cupboard. They're great for snacking on and for tossing into cereals, salads and desserts. They're naturally sweet too, making them a good alternative to sweets or biscuits if you get a craving for something sugary.

MORE TIPS FOR SUPERFOOD SUCCESS

If you find the idea of working a good range of superfoods into your weekly diet a daunting task, there's no need to be anxious. As well as using the easy-to-follow key showing how many portions of fruit and vegetables each

FRUIT & VEGETABLE BOXES

An easy, hassle-free way to buy seasonal fruit and vegetables is to get involved in a local box delivery scheme. Arrange to have a box delivered to your door once or twice a week and you'll find you have no problem eating your 5-a-day and enjoying the super nutrients and health-boosting compounds that they contain. Boxes are usually full of locally grown seasonal fruit and vegetables, so they're fresh and at their best and haven't been transported hundreds or even thousands of kilometres, like most supermarket food. As the seasons change, you'll find the contents of your box changing too, so you'll never get bored with the same old produce. Often when you shop in the supermarket, there's a temptation to throw the same ingredients in the trolley week after week without even thinking about what you're doing, and as a result you can find yourself cooking the same meals week in, week out. When your boxful of fresh produce turns up on your doorstep, however, the contents have been decided for you, and this forces you to experiment and try new things. As well as containing the staples such as carrots, courgettes, potatoes, onions, peppers and salad vegetables, boxes often contain unusual ingredients that you might not buy yourself – whether it's curly kale, an exotic squash, or pak choi or some other peppery oriental greens. There are loads of delicious recipes in this book to help you use both the ordinary and more unusual ingredients that might arrive in your box, but many schemes also provide recipe suggestions with your box to help you cook the ingredients, or explain what to do with an ingredient you might not have come across before. Alternatively, you can look on the Internet to find recipes for any fruit or vegetable you're likely to be given.

recipe provides, there are loads of other sneaky ways of adding these ingredients to your daily meals. And even if you can't make use of the recipes every day, by following these clever tips you'll find you've eaten plenty of superfoods without even noticing.

Drink a 150ml/5fl oz/scant ⅔ cup of fruit juice with your breakfast. Orange juice, pineapple juice and cranberry juice are all great choices as they're packed with vitamin C, which helps to boost the immune system and protect the body from illness – which is a good start to anyone's day. Pineapple juice also gives the digestive system a kick-start, while cranberry juice has natural antibacterial properties and is good for urinary tract infections. If you prefer something less astringent first thing in the morning, try a vegetable juice instead. Tomato or carrot juices are sweet and mild and gentler on the system than fruit juices, while still giving a good hit of nutrients. If you have the time (and a juicer), it's worth making your own fresh juices as they contain more nutrients than the ones you can buy. As soon as the fruit or vegetables have been juiced, the nutrients start to deteriorate, so the fresher the juice the better.

Add a heaped tablespoon of goji berries or a portion of fresh berries or fruit to breakfast cereals or porridge. Soft berries such as raspberries, sliced strawberries or blueberries are great on crunchy cereals such as bran flakes, while slices of nectarine, peach, apple or pear are delicious on healthy cereals such as muesli and granola. Try adding chopped dried fruit such as dates, figs or apricots to porridge oats before you cook them – they add a natural sweetness so you'll need less sugar or honey when you serve the porridge. Alternatively, try puréeing soft berries such as raspberries or strawberries and spooning the purée over the porridge instead of using honey or syrup.

When you fancy a snack – make sure it packs in a good mix of brightly coloured fruit and vegetables (see Superfood Snacking on page 19 for some ideas).

Add extra salad or brightly coloured vegetables to sandwiches, and always serve salad or raw veggie sticks on the side. Crisp lettuce leaves or other peppery salad or herb leaves are always a good choice in sandwiches, as are slices of tomato and cucumber. Sliced chargrilled Mediterranean vegetables such as courgettes, peppers and aubergines are another good, nutritious addition to sandwiches – particularly hot sandwiches such as paninis, or chunky sandwiches made with thick slices of wholegrain bread, ciabatta or focaccia.

On the side, go for a traditional side salad – or be more adventurous with a mixed bean salad or a side of roasted vegetables. If you're in a hurry, a tub of coleslaw – ideally one made with red cabbage and plenty of carrots – is always a great instant standby, and it's good both in a sandwich, as a topping on a jacket potato, or served as a side dish.

When it comes to raw vegetables, you can go for classic crudités, with sticks of cucumber, carrot, celery and sweet pepper. But if you're in a hurry, grab a handful of cherry tomatoes or some sugarsnap peas for a tasty snack.

Add extra vegetables and pulses to curries, casseroles, soups and stir-fries. Throw a can of chopped tomatoes into curries, casseroles or soups, or add a handful or more of chopped vegetables such as carrots, courgettes, peppers or mushrooms to casseroles and chunky soups. Try stirring a handful or so of baby spinach leaves into curries or casseroles about 1 minute before serving until the leaves have just wilted.

Cans of beans are great for adding to curries, casseroles and soups – just drain and rinse, then add to the dish. Lentils, mung beans, chickpeas and black-eyed beans are particularly good in curries, while kidney beans, borlotti beans, cannellini beans and flageolet beans are very good in casseroles and soups. Dried lentils are good added to slow-cooked curries, casseroles and soups. The red ones disintegrate on cooking and can give dishes a lovely thick texture.

Serve at least 2 types of dark green or brightly coloured vegetable with fish, chicken or meat dishes. Choose contrasting colours and flavours for maximum appeal – perhaps steamed carrots and broccoli, roasted red peppers and steamed sugarsnap peas, grilled tomatoes and green bean salad, or perhaps corn on the cob and sautéed spinach.

Make a habit of serving a bowl of salad with every meal – it can make a tasty appetizer or refreshing accompaniment. A classic leafy side salad is always a great choice, but don't be afraid to ring the changes. If there's something new to try, you'll find everyone perking up and wanting to taste some! Add tomatoes, cucumber, spring onions, cooked beetroot, steamed green beans, roasted peppers or fresh herbs. And think about dressings, too, as a way of adding interest to a salad. There are many ready-made ones to choose from or you could make your own.

When you choose a dessert, go for a fruit-based one such as fruit salad, compote or crumble. After all – what could be more satisfying than having a treat and fitting in an extra couple of fruit portions at the same time?

SUPERFOOD SNACKING

Take advantage of those times when you're feeling a little peckish between meals: it's the perfect time to squeeze in a superfood or two. Whether you choose a little something that requires a few minutes of preparation, or you just grab a piece of fruit, all these ideas are quick, simple, tasty and enjoyable. Many of these suggestions are great for popping in a lunchbox, slipping into your bag or having to hand in your desk drawer at work so that when hunger pangs hit you've got your snacks at the ready!

Fresh fruit – any kind will do, whether it's a banana, apple or orange. Whole fruits that aren't too delicate and are easy to eat such as apples and bananas are perfect for snacking on while you're on the run. Pop one in your bag before you leave the house so you've got something to munch on if you get hungry. If you work in an office, why not have a small fruit bowl on your desk? Fill it up on Monday morning with a choice of fruit and dig into it whenever you fancy. For larger fruits such as melon or pineapple, prepare the fruit, cut into bite-sized pieces and store in an airtight container in the fridge, ready to tuck into. If the fruit is already prepared like this, you'll find it so much more tempting to just pick up a piece to munch on than if you have to get out a chopping board and start peeling, slicing and chopping.

Dried fruit – this is an instant energizer, whether it's a handful of sultanas or a few ready-to-eat dried apricots, figs or prunes. It's easy to store and transport too, so ideal for popping into your bag and taking with you when you're going out. You can buy snack-sized bags from the supermarket, although it's more economical to buy a regular large bag of dried fruit, then put a few pieces in a plastic bag yourself for when you're out and about. (Do remember, though, that dried fruit is high in sugar, which isn't great for the teeth or body if eaten in excess. So always think: snacking rather than grazing!) A bag of dried fruit is perfect for your desk drawer at work as well. Keep a bag in there, so when you fancy something sugary you can dip into your dried fruit rather than the office biscuit tin.

Fresh veggie sticks – these can be made from carrots, peppers or celery. They are always delicious – eaten on their own or with a healthy yogurt or hummus dip. Keep some ready in a sealed container in the fridge to tempt you. Veggie sticks can make a good snack-on-the-run as well. Wrap in cling film or foil, or invest in a small container with a tight-fitting lid and pack it with veggie sticks so you've got something in your bag for munching on when you're out and about.

Smoothies – these make a great snack and instant energizer at any time of day. You can buy bottles of ready-made smoothies or you can make them yourself at home. Try out any of the recipes on pages 42–5 and pack in a whopping 2–4 portions per smoothie.

When you fancy a more substantial snack, try mashing half an avocado, season with salt and pepper, add a squeeze of lime juice and spread it on a thick slice of wholegrain toast. It's just as good as peanut butter or melted cheese – but it counts as a portion and provides your body with antioxidant vitamin E and vitamin B6.

Rather than spreading jam on toast, why not crush some fresh berries, stir in a little honey and spread them on toast instead? And on those days when you need a bit of naughty indulgence, you could add a dollop of crème fraîche on top.

If you're after a sugary treat and all you really want is chocolate, then there are ways around it! Make yourself a banana and dark chocolate chip sandwich or try dipping strawberries into melted dark chocolate and leaving it to set before munching.

PACKING YOUR LUNCH THE SUPERFOOD WAY

When you're out and about, eating well can sometimes seem a bit more tricky – but it really shouldn't. There are loads of easy ways to include delicious foods in your packed lunch to help give you a healthy diet. If you take a packed lunch with you regularly, it's worth investing in a lunchbox or containers for salads so you can transport your lunch safely and easily to and from your destination – whether it's school or work. It's good to have one large box that will fit in the whole lunch, such as sandwich, drink, fruit and veggie sticks, but it's also useful to have some smaller containers that fit inside so you could take, for example, a fruit salad one day or a small pot of dressing for a salad another.

It's usually best to make your packed lunch as near to eating time as possible. For most people this means making it in the morning – but some salads, such as a bean salad, would be fine made the evening before and stored in the fridge overnight. If possible, keep your packed lunch in the fridge or somewhere cool to keep the food fresh until lunchtime. If your lunch contains meat, fish or grains such as rice or couscous, then chilling is essential.

Pack wraps and sandwiches with plenty of vegetables such as Ciabattas Filled with Chargrilled Mediterranean Vegetables (see page 108), Smoked Chicken Sandwiches (see page 73) or Chicken, Green Pepper & Mango Wraps (see page 71). When you've made the wrap or sandwich, wrap it tightly in cling film or foil to keep it all together, then pop it in your lunchbox.

Instead of a sandwich, make a healthy salad packed with vegetables and pulses such as Borlotti Bean & Bacon Salad with Artichokes, Green Beans & Cherry Tomatoes (see page 83) or Warm Rice Salad with Spicy Sausage (see page 80). Pack them into a sealed container with a tight-fitting lid, as you don't want dressing leaking out while you transport the salad. Some salads, particularly those with salad leaves, are best dressed just before serving so the leaves don't wilt. Put the dressing into a very small jar or sealed container and put it into your salad box so you can dress the salad just before eating.

A flask of soup with a crusty wholegrain roll makes a great packed lunch – particularly in winter. Make up a batch of vegetable-rich soup such as Creamy Pea & Broad Bean Soup (see page 66) or Thai-spiced Broccoli, Spinach & Cauliflower Soup (see page 64), then pour into a flask and seal tightly.

Include a carton of fruit juice or a small bottle of smoothie in your lunchbox – for a quick, nutrient-packed and energy stabilizing lunchtime boost.

Add a piece of fresh fruit or some dried fruit – it's the perfect snack to nibble on.

Include raw veggie sticks (carrots, celery and pepper) wrapped in cling film to keep them fresh – so that you always have something healthy and easy to hand when you're feeling peckish between meals.

HELPING KIDS TO MAKE THE MOST OF SUPERFOODS

Kids are growing and developing all the time and need all the nutrients they can get to grow and play and to concentrate at school. Since increased vitamin and mineral intake has been found to improve IQ levels in kids, it's vital to encourage them to eat as many vegetables and pieces of fruit as possible. Some kids love their fruit and vegetables while others are less than keen. But the great news is that there are loads of ways you can help and encourage your kids to eat more healthily. It's also important to remember that the patterns and behaviours we learn in childhood tend to carry on into adulthood, so it really is best to help your kids to eat healthily from the start so they don't have to try to kick bad habits as they grow up. Here are some useful tips to encourage your kids to eat more fruit and vegetables – one of the main sources of superfood nutrients in their diet.

Ask your kids to help you choose the fruit and vegetables on the shopping list. Start off by making a list of all the fruit and vegetables they like. Then make another list of the ones they've tried but don't like, and a third list of all the fruit and vegetables they've never tried – this will probably include unusual items such as sharon fruit and okra as well as some more common candidates that have just never taken their fancy, such as beetroot or aubergines. Every week try to include lots from the first list and then ask them to try something from the other two lists, even if it's just a little taste.

Be prepared to experiment. Younger kids are sometimes put off by the texture of fruit and vegetables rather than the taste. So you might discover that they like some fruit and vegetables when they're prepared or cooked in a different way to usual, for example puréeing fruit, mashing peas instead of just boiling them (as in Grilled Salmon on Chilli Pea Mash with Roasted Squash, see page 135) or serving baked apples or poached pears for a snack or dessert instead of a piece of raw fruit.

When you're out shopping, ask them what looks nice and what appeals to them. If they point to a pumpkin or a punnet of blueberries, why not buy them and then talk about what you'll make them into for dinner that evening?

Get them involved in the kitchen. If your kids have enjoyed helping to make a meal, they're more likely to want to sit down and try it. (And even if that doesn't work, at least you're furnishing them with the life-skill of knowing how to prepare and cook a dish!)

Tell your kids about the ingredients as you're cooking to make them interesting. Knowing that carrots are full of beta-carotene to help their eyes see better, that oranges will help fight off bugs and colds, and that spinach is full of iron to make their blood strong might make all the difference to a reluctant child.

SECRET SUPERFOODS

For some people, eating healthy ingredients – no matter how tasty you make them – can seem to be something of a chore and you may need to resort to tactics of stealth and subterfuge to pack in those portions every day. Below are a few ideas to help you hide those essential superfoods so that they can't be seen on the plate!

Vegetable mash – rather than making plain potato mash, add other vegetables as well. Substitute classic mash with half carrots or roast squash and half potato, or a mixture of carrots, celeriac and potato. Alternatively, stir some sliced sautéed leeks into mashed potatoes, or stir baby spinach leaves into the mash about 1 minute before serving until just wilted.

Soups are a great place to hide vegetables. Any vegetables are good, but the following are particularly popular: onions, leeks, skinned tomatoes, carrots, squash, peppers and parsnips. Just cook until soft, then blend until smooth.

When you make a bolognese sauce, chop carrots, peppers and onions very finely, stir them in and simmer with the sauce. Once cooked, they'll virtually vanish.

Purée or crush fresh fruit such as berries, peaches, mango, pineapple or banana, or cooked fruits such as stewed apple, rhubarb or gooseberries or baked plums or apricots – spoon over ice cream or desserts as a sauce, or stir into whipped cream or a mixture of whipped cream and yogurt to make an indulgent dessert. Alternatively, freeze in ice lolly moulds and serve them as a healthy summer treat.

Tempt your kids by making fruit and vegetables seem like an appealing treat. Cut up carrots into bite-sized sticks and offer them with a creamy yogurt dip for dunking, or put a bowl of sweet cherry tomatoes in front of them when they're watching TV for little hands to dip into.

Take advantage of the times your kids are most hungry by feeding them healthy food first – try to ensure you have some healthy snacks already prepared so there is a quick and easy option available in the fridge for them to grab. At dinner, why not serve a salad first, when they're at their hungriest and, therefore, most likely to eat it?

Always serve ice cream with at least 1 portion of fruit – whether it's a sliced peach or banana, a handful of fresh berries or a couple of heaped spoonfuls of crushed mango or pineapple.

If all else fails and you're still facing resistance, you'll have to become devious and hide some superfoods in their favourite meals! (See the box above for some ideas.)

KNOW YOUR SUPERFOODS

Every single food contains its own unique combination of health-giving nutrients and compounds, making them superfoods for your body in so many different ways. The following pages take the mystery out of which foods contain what, and how they can help you to be better, brighter and healthier.

FRUIT

All types of fruits (and vegetables) are packed with nutrients, including vitamins, minerals and fibre, and are naturally low in fat. They're also brimming with antioxidant compounds known as phytochemicals, which have numerous health benefits. You should aim to eat at least 5 portions of fruit and vegetables every day – a total of 400g/14oz. If you fancy something sweet, choose fruit rather than foods containing sugar, such as biscuits, cakes, sweets and sugary drinks, which are often high in calories but have no beneficial nutrients and can often cause tooth decay.

APPLES Rich in soluble fibre, which helps to lower blood cholesterol levels, and insoluble fibre, required by the digestive system, apples also contain malic and tartaric acids, which inhibit fermentation in the intestines. They are a good source of vitamin C, which is needed for a healthy immune system. In addition, apples contain the phytochemical quercetin, which is thought to help reduce inflammatory and allergic reactions in the body. According to research, the regular consumption of apples is associated with a reduced risk of cancer, heart disease, asthma and type 2 diabetes. Besides being a popular snack and lunchbox item, apples make wonderful desserts when cooked in pies and crumbles, when baked, or when stewed until soft in a little fruit juice and then puréed to make apple sauce. Also try adding grated apples to cereals or porridge to sweeten them instead of sugar. For an interesting apple-based savoury recipe, try Marinated Pork Chops with Roasted Apples, Squash & Red Onions (see page 123).

APRICOTS Fresh apricots are a great source of the antioxidant nutrients beta-carotene and vitamin C, while the dried variety also provides iron, which is needed to form haemoglobin, the oxygen-carrying component of the blood. Both fresh and dried apricots are also a good source of insoluble fibre, which aids healthy digestion, and potassium, which helps to control the body's fluid balance. Apricots can be eaten fresh or cooked, and are delicious when chopped and served with yogurt or crème fraîche. Dried apricots (for health reasons choose the unsulphured variety) go well in dried fruit salads and crumbles or can add a touch of sweetness to savoury dishes such as meat or vegetable casseroles.

BANANAS An excellent source of potassium, which helps to control blood pressure, bananas are also a good source of fibre. On top of this they contain vitamin B6, are high in carbohydrates and the energy boost given by their high sugar levels make them the perfect snack. They can be chopped or mashed and added to cereals, homemade cakes and breads as a natural sweetener. They can also be used to thicken smoothies or as a sandwich filling with peanut butter and honey.

BLACKCURRANTS Packed with immune-boosting vitamin C and rich in antioxidants thought to combat a number of illnesses including heart disease, cancer, Alzheimer's disease and diabetes, blackcurrants are tiny fruit with a mighty health-punch. With a strong, sharp flavour they need sweetening, so, to avoid adding excess sugar to your diet, try combining them with naturally sweet fruits such as pears in crumbles and pies.

BLUEBERRIES Full of potent phytochemicals called anthocyanidins, blueberries are regarded as an immune-boosting superfood, thought to protect against cataracts, glaucoma, varicose veins, haemorrhoids, heart disease and cancer. The antioxidants in blueberries have also been found to protect the brain and may reduce the effects of conditions such as Alzheimer's disease or dementia. Delicious eaten raw just as a snack or in fruit salads, blueberries are also superb in muffins, pies and pancake fillings.

CHERRIES A good source of immune-boosting vitamin C, cherries also contain various B vitamins and the mineral potassium, required for normal fluid balance. They also possess phytochemicals known as anthocyanins, which are thought to reduce inflammation and protect against a number of diseases associated with ageing. The anthocyanins give cherries their colour, so the darker the fruit, the better. Cherries are also reputed to have natural painkilling properties and are traditionally used to alleviate gout by moderating uric acid levels. Eat these wonderful summer fruits fresh, or pit them and add to pies, compotes and fruit cakes. You can also buy dried cherries, which can be used to add antioxidant power to mueslis and breakfast cereals, as in the Dried Cherry Granola with Fresh Fruit (see page 47).

CITRUS FRUITS A large study has shown that children with asthma experience significantly less wheezing if they eat a diet high in citrus fruits, which are rich in vitamin C. Citrus fruits also contain the soluble fibre pectin, which helps to lower high blood cholesterol. They're also a rich source of phytochemicals, including carotenoids, flavonoids, glucarates and limonoids, which are all thought to promote heart health and protect against various cancers.

Oranges are a great source of folate, which is important for pregnant women or women who are planning to conceive, while lemons have a cleansing effect on the body. And if you're put off by the tartness of grapefruit, you might be encouraged to eat it if you're on a diet, because it helps the body to burn fat. Try using citrus juices to flavour cakes and puddings. Also, serve lemon or lime wedges for squeezing over dishes, and use slices to add a zing to mineral water. Finally, no fruit salad would be complete without a handful of chopped orange or satsuma segments.

CRANBERRIES These tasty fruits contain natural antibacterial properties, making them a great remedy for urinary tract infections such as cystitis. They also contain quinine, which is an effective liver detoxifier. To balance the tartness of fresh cranberries, combine them with other fruits such as oranges, mango, pineapple and pears or eat them chopped with a little added fruit juice or honey. If you've never cooked with cranberries before, try Upside-down Cranberry, Apple & Cherry Tart (see page 177).

DATES Rich in natural sugars and insoluble fibre, dates help to support energy levels and a healthy digestive system. They're a rich source of potassium, which helps to control blood pressure; iron, which is essential for the production of haemoglobin in the blood; and magnesium and manganese – minerals that are needed by the nervous system. Fresh dates can be eaten as a snack, added to sandwiches (try cottage cheese and date) or stuffed with nuts such as walnuts. Chopped dried dates make a tasty addition to breakfast cereals or can be used to sweeten salads, tagines, muffins and cereal bars.

GRAPES These are high in carbohydrates and are easily digested, making them a perfect energy or convalescing food. They contain the phytochemical quercetin, which is thought to help reduce inflammation and the risk of heart attack and stroke. All grapes contain ellagic acid, and dark-skinned ones are rich in the potent antioxidants resveratrol and anthocyanins, both of which are believed to help protect against various cancers. Grapes also have a cleansing and mild laxative effect, which is attributed to their high potassium and magnesium content. They can make attractive additions to fruit salads and tarts. They also taste good when added to green salads or when served with cheese as a dessert or snack.

KIWI FRUIT Bursting with immune-boosting vitamin C, kiwi fruit are also rich in the antioxidant vitamin E, which helps to protect the body against diseases such as cancer, heart disease and Alzheimer's disease. They also contain the phytochemical lutein, which has a positive effect on eye health, reducing the risk of cataracts and macular degeneration. The fruit is a good source of fibre (for healthy digestion), potassium (to help support the body's fluid balance) and magnesium (which is essential for bones, nerves and muscles). Kiwis can be added to fruit salads such as Tropical Fruit Salad (see page 53), tossed into green salads or sliced to decorate cheesecakes and other desserts.

MANGOES High in vitamins B6, C and E, mangoes are also a good source of fibre and the minerals iron, copper and magnesium. In addition, they are rich in beta-carotene, which is believed to help build up resistance to respiratory tract infections and aid immune function. To prepare mangoes, slice down either side of the stone, then remove the skin. Unripe ones are often used in chutneys, relishes and pickles.

MELONS A good source of vitamin C, melons have a diuretic and cleansing effect on the system and are good for the skin. Orange-fleshed melons such as cantaloupe are particularly high in beta-carotene, which is an antioxidant nutrient and immune-booster. Watermelon contains the phytochemical lycopene, which has been associated with a reduced risk of macular degeneration and cancers of the prostate, lung, bladder, cervix and skin. Melons can be eaten for breakfast or as an appetizer; they can also be stuffed with chopped fruit to make a delicious and nutrient-packed dessert such as Fruit-filled Melons (see page 159).

PAPAYAS This sweet, tropical fruit contains both vitamin C and beta-carotene – antioxidants that boost the immune system and slow down ageing. Papaya is also a good source of folate, potassium and vitamin E as well as containing the enzyme papain, which aids protein digestion. However, levels of papain reduce as the fruit ripens. To enjoy fresh papaya, simply cut it in half lengthways, remove the seeds and eat the flesh with a spoon. Papaya is a good addition to smoothies along with other fruit, and works well in fruit salads.

PEACHES & NECTARINES A single nectarine contains an adult's entire recommended daily allowance of vitamin C. Peaches and nectarines also contain potassium, which helps to regulate blood pressure, and phytochemicals that protect against various cancers and help maintain a healthy heart. The nutrients in these fruits are also good for skin, lung, digestive and eye health. Eat them raw or cooked in pies, turnovers and crêpes.

PEARS Rich in soluble fibre, which helps to lower blood cholesterol and protect the heart, pears also contain vitamin C and the mineral potassium, which helps to regulate the body's fluid balance. The levulose sugar found in pears makes them a good choice of fruit for diabetics, as this is more easily tolerated than other types of fruit sugar. Try adding chopped pears to green salads, serve them with cheese as a dessert, poach them in a little apple juice or mix grated pears into muesli, granola and porridge for breakfast.

PINEAPPLE A good source of vitamin C, pineapple also contains potassium, for regulating fluid balance, and manganese, which is needed for skin, bone and cartilage formation. It also contains a compound called bromelain, which is a protein-digesting enzyme with anti-inflammatory properties. Serve chopped pineapple with yogurt or simmer it in a little maple syrup until brown. Add it to fruit salads, especially those containing other exotic fruits such as papaya, kiwi and mango, or use it to jazz up savoury foods such as pizza, rice or cottage cheese. Pineapple is often used as the sweet element in oriental sweet-and-sour dishes.

PLUMS Their different colours, from yellow through to red and dark purple, indicate that the fruits contain different phytochemicals. Darker-skinned plums contain higher levels of those phytochemicals that are believed to protect against cancers by neutralizing free radicals in the body. They are a good source of vitamin C and beta-carotene, and contain vitamin B2, which promotes healthy skin, hair and nails. For a lovely dessert, poach plums in a little red wine, fruit juice or a splash of water and a sprinkling of brown sugar. You can also stew or bake pitted plums and serve them with yogurt and honey or make them into an ice cream or sorbet such as Pear & Plum Sorbet (see page 167). Plums are also available in their dried form as prunes.

RASPBERRIES These wonderfully sweet fruits contain folate, which is important during pregnancy and for women trying to conceive; manganese, required for healthy skin, cartilage and bones; and fibre, for an efficient digestive system. They also contain vitamin C and the phytochemicals anthocyanins and ellagic acid, which are associated with a reduced risk of cancer. They have natural antimicrobial properties and may help to prevent the growth of *Candida albicans*, which is responsible for yeast infections such as thrush. Raspberries are believed to help cleanse the digestive system and have traditionally been used to treat diarrhoea, indigestion and rheumatism. They are highly versatile. Besides being delicious when eaten straight off the cane, they combine well with other berries to make fillings for pancakes and crêpes, and can be enjoyed in pies and smoothies or as jam.

STRAWBERRIES This popular fruit is an excellent source of immune-boosting vitamin C, and provides a useful source of folate and the minerals iodine and manganese. Strawberries also contain phytochemicals, including anthocyanins, which have anti-cancer and anti-inflammatory properties, and ellagic acid, which has been associated with decreased rates of cancer. For a deliciously rich strawberry-based recipe, treat yourself to Mixed-berry Eton Mess (see page 158). Other ways to use these multipurpose berries is in tarts, pancake fillings, roulades, smoothies and milkshakes, whizzed up in yogurt or fromage frais to make creamy desserts, served on top of cakes or waffles, or added sliced to mixed green salads. The options are endless!

VEGETABLES

ARTICHOKES (GLOBE) Rich in potassium, which helps to control fluid balance, vitamin C and fibre, artichokes also contain a compound called cynarin, extracts of which have been found to protect the liver. Serve this vegetable as an appetizer with a little lemon juice and olive oil, or as an accompaniment to a meal.

ASPARAGUS A traditional remedy for kidney problems, asparagus contains the amino acid asparagine, which, when combined with the potassium content in this vegetable, gives asparagus its diuretic effect. It contains many other nutrients, including beta-carotene, vitamins C and K, folate, several B vitamins and fibre. Serve it as a side dish with a squeeze of lemon juice or chopped in pasta dishes, omelettes and quiches.

AVOCADOS Although relatively high in fat, avocados are rich in good monounsaturated fats, which help to lower cholesterol. They are also a great source of vitamin E – a powerful antioxidant – and provide vitamin B6, required for the health of the nervous system, as well as being an excellent food for the skin. A good source of biotin, avocados help to prevent dry skin and brittle hair and nails. Add avocados to salads and sandwiches, blend them into homemade salad dressings for extra richness, spread them on bread instead of butter, or use them to make dips such as traditional guacamole or salsas, such as Chicken Fajitas with Avocado Salsa (see page 112).

BEETROOT The compound responsible for the deep red colour of beetroot is known as betacyanin, which is an antioxidant that enhances liver detoxification. This vegetable is also rich in folate, which is essential for preventing birth defects; iron; and manganese, which is required for healthy skin, bones and cartilage. Beetroot are usually eaten boiled or roasted, and in Eastern Europe cold beetroot soup (borscht) is a popular dish. Raw grated beetroot is delicious in salads and sandwiches and beetroot juice blends well with other vegetable juices such as carrot and celery for a healthy cocktail.

BROCCOLI As a member of the Brassicaceae family, broccoli contains potent anti-cancer compounds, including sulforaphane, which helps to neutralize potentially cancer-forming substances in the body. It also contains indole-3-carbinol, which inactivates oestrone, a dangerous form of oestrogen that is associated with breast cancer. Broccoli also provides useful amounts of immune-boosting beta-carotene and vitamin C; folate, which helps to reduce levels of homocysteine in the blood (high levels of which can increase the risk of heart disease); calcium, for healthy bones and teeth; iron, for red blood cell haemoglobin production, and the mineral zinc. As an accompaniment to main meals, broccoli is best steamed rather than boiled to maintain its nutritional value. It can also be added to stir-fries, such as Stir-fried Chicken (see page 115), or to pasta dishes or soups.

CABBAGE This is from the same vegetable family as broccoli and contains similar cancer-fighting compounds such as sulforaphane and indoles. Cabbage is also a good source of vitamin C and folate, which is needed for healthy cell division and is particularly important for pregnant women and women planning to conceive. Cabbage juice has had remarkable success in the healing of stomach and duodenal ulcers, which has been put down to a compound in raw cabbage that is known as S-Methylmethionine. Try finely shredded cabbage added to stir-fries, use raw in salads, make a delicious coleslaw – a perfect sandwich filling, or use the leaves in more creative ways to make wrappings for rice parcels.

CARROTS Bright orange carrots are rich in protective beta-carotene, vital for the health of the eyes and immune system. People who eat plenty of fruits and vegetables high in beta-carotene appear to be at lower risk of cataracts and macular degeneration. This popular vegetable is highly versatile either grated raw in salads or cooked in casseroles, soups and stir-fries. Carrot cake is also very popular for its perfectly moist texture.

CAULIFLOWER Packed with phytochemicals that are believed to protect against certain cancers, cauliflower also contains immune-boosting vitamin C, and vitamin K, which helps with blood clotting. Serve steamed as a vegetable accompaniment with fish or meat, in curries such as chickpea and cauliflower, or raw in salads. Try it in Macaroni Cheese with Ham, Cauliflower & Broccoli (see page 141).

CELERY This vegetable contains several active compounds including phalides, which may help to lower cholesterol, and coumarins, which may be useful in cancer prevention. The vegetable's diuretic effect is due to its high sodium and potassium content. Celery is also rich in vitamins C and K. A few quick serving ideas include adding chopped celery to soups and salads, making vegetable crudités or adding some freshly squeezed celery juice to carrot juice for extra flavour.

COURGETTES The nutritional value of courgettes is modest, and most of these nutrients, which include manganese and vitamin C, are found in the dark green skin. Add them to your favourite stews and casseroles or roast them with other chopped vegetables such as red onions, peppers and squash.

FENNEL A good source of vitamin C, potassium, manganese and fibre, fennel is also rich in phytochemicals including rutin, which helps to strengthen blood capillaries; quercetin, which has anti-inflammatory activity; and kaempferol glycosides, which are thought to help protect against certain cancers. Fennel also contains fibre, for digestive health, and folate, which helps to prevent birth defects. This crunchy, flavoursome vegetable is delicious when grated in salads, on pizzas, or in sandwiches, or when sautéed or braised and served as a side dish. Try it in Creamy Chicken Baked with Fennel & Carrots (see page 116).

GARLIC There are at least 33 sulphur-containing compounds in fresh garlic, including allicin, alliin and ajoene. Allicin, which has potent antibacterial and antifungal properties, is released only when garlic is cut or crushed. However, it degrades very quickly, so to reap its benefits, eat garlic raw and as soon as possible after chopping. It is the sulphur compounds in garlic that are also responsible for its positive effect on the circulatory system – reducing blood pressure and cholesterol and the risk of heart attack and stroke. In addition, garlic is an excellent source of manganese, and a good source of selenium. Nothing beats garlic as a flavour-enhancer. Use it in soups, sauces and casseroles, crush it and add to salad dressings, or, for a milder flavour, use whole, unpierced garlic cloves.

KALE This crinkly dark green leaf from the cabbage family is a great source of fibre for digestion and is packed with antioxidant and anti-inflammatory flavonoids, which are thought to help combat a number of cancers. It is also a good source of vitamin C and K. It's a great accompaniment to any main meal, steamed for just a few minutes and served as it is or tossed with a little butter.

MANGETOUTS & SUGARSNAP PEAS Mangetouts and sugarsnap peas contain potassium, which helps to regulate fluid balance, vitamins C and B6, and fibre. They are also a good source of beta-carotene and lutein, which protect against cataract development and macular degeneration. Unlike green peas, the pods of these pea varieties are edible. Stir-fry them with other vegetables, or add them to green salads.

MUSHROOMS A good source of B vitamins, which are important for a healthy nervous system, mushrooms also contain useful amounts of the minerals potassium, copper, manganese, phosphorous and zinc. White mushrooms are the most widely consumed, although there are many other varieties, including oyster, porcini and shiitake. Serve them in salads or add them to sauces, stews and stir-fries.

ONIONS & LEEKS Like garlic, these vegetables belong to the Allium family, consumption of which has been associated with a reduced risk of prostate cancer in men. They also contain compounds called saponins, which prevent cancer cells from multiplying, and allyl sulphides, which help to increase the production of cancer-protecting antioxidant enzymes in the body. Onions contain the phytochemical quercetin, which is thought to have an anti-inflammatory effect and also help reduce the risk of heart attack and stroke. While onions are a household staple, leeks, their milder cousin, can be used in a similar way to add flavour to recipes, or be steamed, pan-fried or baked and served as an accompaniment.

PEPPERS Red, orange and yellow peppers are very rich in vitamin C. They are also high in immune-boosting beta-carotene and the carotenoids lutein and zeaxanthin, which are thought to help protect against cataracts and macular degeneration. Red peppers are one of the few foods that contain lycopene, the consumption of which has been associated with a reduced incidence of cancers of the prostate, lung, bladder, cervix and skin. Peppers look and taste great in many dishes, including salads, stir-fries, quiches, omelettes and grain-based meals. They can also be blended and added to dressings, stuffed or served as a crudité with other vegetables.

PUMPKIN & SQUASH Packed with complex carbohydrates, these vegetables are excellent energy foods. They are also a great source of beta-carotene, required for immune health, and contain valuable amounts of vitamins C, B1, B5, B6 and folate, and the minerals manganese and copper. Pumpkin and squash are delicious when baked and stuffed with grains and other vegetables or when chopped and added to casseroles and curries. The cooked flesh can also be puréed, making these vegetables ideal foods for babies.

SPINACH This dark green vegetable is rich in a broad range of nutrients, including folate, which is important for its role in preventing birth defects; iron for haemoglobin production; vitamin C and beta-carotene for immune health; and the minerals calcium, magnesium, manganese and potassium. It also contains the carotenoid lutein, associated with eye health, and many antioxidants that help to fight the damaging effects of free radicals associated with cancer, heart disease and the ageing process. Spinach cooks quickly and is best steamed for a few minutes and then tossed in olive oil and lemon juice, or sautéed. It can also be added to casseroles, curries, stuffings, omelettes and quiches. Baby leaf spinach is good eaten raw in salads.

OFF THE BEATEN TRACK

There are a number of more unusual ingredients and supplements that also deserve the superfood status. You can find most of these in health food stores, and some larger supermarkets.

Goji berries These small Himalayan berries are packed with beta-carotene and vitamin C, as well as substantial quantities of B vitamins and vitamin E. They are reputed to protect against heart disease and cancer, as well as boost immunity and brain activity. Try them as a snack or scatter on cereal, porridge or fruit salads.

Seaweed A plant-like organism of the algae family, there are numerous types of edible seaweed that are packed with nutrients. They are a good source of calcium, vitamin C, iodine and potent antioxidants. Seaweed is reputed to help thyroid function, combat some cancers and may prevent inflammation that can contribute to ailments such as arthritis, celiac disease and asthma. Enjoy nori sheets wrapped around sushi, kelp in salads or simmered in miso soup, or dried seaweed flaked over rice. Be aware that too much seaweed can also cause problems, so as with every food and nutrient – balance and moderation is the key word.

Spirulina A natural algae, spirulina is usually available in powder form from health food stores. It is an excellent source of protein and iron. Rich in chlorophyll, which is reputed to boost the immune system and help detox the blood, spirulina is also a good source of B vitamins and vitamins C, D and E. Try stirring a spoonful into smoothies.

Chia seeds Native to Mexico and Guatemala, these seeds are rich in omega-3 fatty acids and are also a good source of calcium, manganese and phosphorous. They are reputed to boost energy, stabilize blood sugar, aid digestion and lower cholesterol. They have very little flavour and are good sprinkled over salads. The ground form is great stirred into smoothies.

Acai Native to South America, this inch-long reddish purple berry has been touted for its antioxidant properties, which are thought to help combat diseases such as cancer and heart disease. In particular they contain the phytochemicals flavonoids and anthocyanins.

Baobab fruit Almost 50 per cent fibre for good digestion and a source of 14 vitamins and minerals, this Sub-Saharan fruit is said to be good for mood, stress, skin health and the immune system, as well as having anti-ageing properties.

Wheatgrass Usually available as small shots of fresh juice from health food stores and juice bars, this intensely flavoured juice is claimed to be the ultimate detoxer. If you're new to wheatgrass juice, sip your shot slowly as its effects can be quite potent.

Hemp seeds Technically, these sunflower-sized seeds are actually a fruit. They are a good source of protein, essential fatty acids, disease-fighting antioxidants and minerals, including zinc, calcium and iron. Use them just as you would other seeds – in breads, sprinkled on salads, or added to muesli.

TOMATOES Probably the most outstanding feature of the tomato is its lycopene content – a phytochemical thought to help protect against various cancers, including those of the prostate, lung, bladder, cervix and skin. While cooking or processing fruit and vegetables generally reduces their benefits, cooked or tinned tomatoes actually have increased levels of lycopene – so making them a better option when you're trying to increase your intake of this valuable compound. Tomatoes are also a very good source of vitamins C and K and beta-carotene. Tomatoes can be used in countless ways: add them to salads, sandwiches and soups, use in salsas and dips, and to make tomato or pasta sauces, or drink tomato juice as part of a healthy breakfast.

WATERCRESS Legitimately endorsed as a superfood, peppery-tasting watercress is packed with nutrients, including vitamin C, beta-carotene and iron. It is also an excellent source of calcium and magnesium, for healthy bones and teeth; sulphur, which is good for the hair, skin and nails; and a phytochemical called phenethyl isothiocyanate, or PEITC, which has been shown to increase the body's potential to resist certain cancer-causing agents. This leafy green vegetable can also be enjoyed in salads and sandwiches, or blended with fresh basil, pine nuts, olive oil and garlic to make a zingy and nutritious homemade pesto.

NUTS & SEEDS

ALMONDS Rich in the good monounsaturated fats for a healthy heart, almonds also contain plant sterols, which help to reduce the risk of heart disease by actively competing with the absorption of cholesterol in the blood. They are an excellent source of folate, which protects against birth defects; calcium and magnesium, for strong bones and teeth; and the antioxidant vitamin E. In addition, they contain a natural pain-killing agent called salicylate. The blanched form of this health-giving nut can be added to all manner of meals, including stir-fries, salads, and rice.

BRAZIL NUTS These stocky, creamy nuts are an extremely rich source of the mineral selenium, which is thought to support the immune system, aid thyroid function, boost fertility and help wounds heal. Your body only needs a small amount of selenium – too much selenium can have a negative impact on your health. Just 3 or 4 brazil nuts a day will provide you with all the selenium you require.

PEANUTS A good source of protein, peanuts also provide fibre, vitamin E and folate. They are rich in monounsaturated fats, and contain the phytochemical resveratrol, which is thought to help reduce the risk of "bad" cholesterol in the blood. Peanuts are a staple ingredient in many cuisines, including African and Indonesian. Sprinkle peanuts on to salads or add them to sweet and savoury dishes.

PUMPKIN SEEDS Rich in zinc, which is important for normal growth in children, healthy sexual function and the immune system, pumpkin seeds also contain vitamin E and the minerals iron, copper, manganese and magnesium. They are rich in essential fatty acids, which, coupled with their zinc content, are believed to promote prostate health in men. To maintain their nutritional value, pumpkin seeds are best eaten raw. Toss them into salads, sprinkle on to casseroles, soups and cereals or enjoy as a snack.

SESAME SEEDS These tiny seeds are mega-rich in calcium and also an excellent source of copper, manganese, magnesium, iron and zinc, as well as the essential fatty acids needed for healthy skin. Additionally they contain two unique substances, sesamin and sesamol, that have been found to lower blood pressure and cholesterol. They have a slightly bitter taste, but their flavour can be improved by lightly toasting them in a dry pan over a medium heat. Use them in baking or sprinkle them as a garnish.

WALNUTS Rich in healthy fats that can help to reduce "bad" cholesterol levels in the blood, walnuts also contain protein and the phytochemical known as ellagic acid, which possesses anti-cancer properties. The B vitamins and manganese found in walnuts make them an excellent brain food. Mix crushed walnuts into yogurt and top with honey or add them to baked goods and stuffing recipes.

CARBOHYDRATES

High-carb foods such as bread, pasta, potatoes and rice provide our bodies with a source of energy and keep us going. They are essential for good health and should make up about one-third of what we eat every day. They are low in fat and high in fibre, B vitamins and various minerals. Where possible, try to choose wholegrain varieties, such as wholemeal bread and pasta and brown rice, which are richer in nutrients and fibre than the white versions and keep you feeling fuller for longer. Make sure you get enough carbs by including at least one carbohydrate-rich food with each main meal – perhaps wholegrain cereal at breakfast, a sandwich at lunch, and a rice or potato-based dish for dinner.

BARLEY Rich in fibre, barley is also a good source of copper, selenium and zinc, and vitamin B6 – essential for the health of the nervous and immune systems. Barley also has a very low glycaemic index (GI) and so provides a great source of slow-releasing energy. Barley can be used as a delicious breakfast, added to soups and stews for extra flavour and as a rice substitute.

BEANS & PULSES Lentils, chickpeas and cannellini, haricot, red kidney, flageolet and butter beans are an excellent source of both insoluble and soluble fibre. They also have a low GI, so provide a good source of slow-releasing carbohydrate, which can be useful for balancing blood sugar levels. In addition, they contain folate, manganese, iron and molybdenum and are a good source of protein. Unlike animal products, beans and pulses are very low in fat and, therefore, make a great supplement if you're cutting down on meat. Add these highly versatile ingredients to soups such as Chunky Lentil & Coconut Soup (see page 64), use them to make dips such as Cannellini Bean & Red Pepper Dip (see page 108) or concoct healthy curries from them such as Lentil & Coconut Milk Curry (see page 153).

BULGUR WHEAT Bulgur is made from steamed, hulled and cracked wheat berries. It is rich in insoluble fibre to help maintain a regular digestive system, and is also a good source of B vitamins, which are important for metabolism and the nervous system. It also provides slow-releasing energy into the bloodstream. Bulgur is best when added to stews and soups, used instead of rice in pilaffs, or made into a quick tabbouleh salad.

OATS A good source of energy-giving carbohydrates, oats are also high in B vitamins and vitamin E and the minerals calcium, magnesium, iron and zinc. They contain soluble fibre, which helps to sustain blood sugar levels, making them an ideal breakfast food. The fibre in oats has also been linked to heart health and the lowering of cholesterol. Besides using them to make porridge, oats make wonderful crumble toppings or homemade flapjacks. Oatmeal can be used as a thickener in sauces.

QUINOA Often referred to as the ultimate supergrain, this South American grain has been eaten for thousands of years and was recognized for its nutritional benefits by the Incas. It is the only grain considered to be a whole protein, containing all 8 amino acids, and is also rich in other nutrients including iron, magnesium, lysene and vitamin B2. Enjoy it as you would rice in pilaffs, stews and salads.

SPELT Often favoured by those who are unable to tolerate wheat or gluten – the gluten in spelt has been found to be easier to digest than that found in wheat. This grain is a good source of carbohydrate and fibre and also contains B vitamins, iron and calcium. Use it as you would rice in pilaffs and salads.

DAIRY PRODUCTS

Aim to eat some dairy produce, such as milk, yogurt or cheese, every day. It's a great source of calcium, which is important for strong bones and teeth, as well as other nutrients, including protein, vitamins A, B12 and D. If you're unable to eat dairy foods, there are plenty of substitutes, such as soya, oat and rice milk, soya yogurt and soya cheese – although their nutrient values will differ to dairy.

MILK Rich in calcium, which is important for healthy bones and teeth, milk also contains good quantities of vitamin B12, which is needed by the blood and nerve cells, and vitamin B2, which the body needs to turn food into energy. Children should drink full-fat milk up to the age of 5, but after that age semi-skimmed or skimmed milk will provide all the nutrients they need.

YOGURT A good source of calcium and vitamins B2 and B12, yogurt that is labelled "live" contains beneficial bacteria, which are vital for the health of the digestive system. Some people who cannot digest milk are able to tolerate yogurt. Eat yogurt as a simple dessert with fresh fruit and nuts, use it to make salad dressings or add it to recipes instead of high-fat cream.

PROTEIN

Protein-rich foods, such as meat, fish, eggs, tofu and other soya products, are essential in a healthy diet. The body needs protein to maintain and repair the body's cells, as well as for the proper functioning of the entire system, including hormones, enzymes and antibodies. Try to choose low-fat cuts of meat and aim to eat 2 portions of fish a week, including 1 portion of oily fish. If you're vegetarian, you can get all the protein you need from eggs and dairy produce, or plant-based sources of protein such as beans and pulses, grains and tofu.

EGGS One of the few dietary sources of vitamin D, which is required for the absorption of calcium, eggs also provide vitamins A, E and B2 and are an excellent source of vitamin B12. They're also rich in lecithin, which is needed for normal brain function. You can now also buy eggs that are rich in healthy omega-3 fats. Eggs are the centrepiece of a range of recipes, including omelettes, frittatas (such as the Spinach & Roasted Red Pepper Frittata; see page 147), soufflés and cakes.

OILY FISH Fish such as salmon, mackerel, sardines, anchovies and fresh tuna are rich in omega-3 fatty acids, which help to thin the blood and lower blood pressure. Children who eat oily fish may have a much lower risk of getting asthma. It is thought that a high intake of oily fish may reduce the risk of age-related dementia. The canning process destroys these healthy fats in tuna, so buy fresh if you can; salmon is not similarly affected. Try oily fish in salads, as a sandwich filling, on toast as a pâté or with pasta.

PRAWNS Although prawns contain healthy omega-3 fats, they are also relatively high in cholesterol compared with other food, so eat them in moderation if you are watching your cholesterol levels. Prawns are also a good source of vitamin B12 and the minerals selenium, iron and zinc, all of which aid the immune system. Prawns can be cooked in a variety of ways – grilled, stir-fried or steamed – and then added to salads, soups and rice and pasta dishes. For a simple prawn dish, try Zingy Prawn Salad (see page 93).

RED MEAT Although red meat can be high in saturated fat and so should be eaten in moderation, it is a useful source of iron, which is essential for the body's production of haemoglobin, and zinc, which is essential for growth, development and maintaining healthy reproductive and immune systems.

TOFU Made from soya beans, tofu is high in protein and low in calories and fat. It is also a good source of calcium and contains oestrogen-like compounds called isoflavones, which may help to reduce the symptoms of menopause. Tofu is good for vegans and vegetarians and can replace meat and dairy products in most recipes. Experiment with plain, smoked and marinated tofu for variety.

NATURE'S PHARMACY

With nature's bounty at hand, there's no need to reach for the medicine cabinet or vitamin bottle when your body requires a boost. Every food in its natural state contains a fabulous wealth of vitamins, minerals and nutrients to give your body the health injection it needs. Outlined below is an easy-to-use, quick reference guide for all the key nutrients, what they can do for you, and where to find them in your kitchen or local store. Use the previous Know Your Superfoods section on pages 24–38 to see which foods contain the particular nutrients listed below.

VITAMIN A Important for healthy eyes, skin, lungs, digestion and the immune system, this vitamin is available only from animal sources such as meat, eggs and dairy products. However, beta-carotene, which is found in orange fruits and vegetables such as carrots, mangoes and apricots, can be converted to vitamin A in the body.

B VITAMINS This family of vitamins includes thiamine (B1), riboflavin (B2), niacin (B3), pantothenic acid (B5) and pyridoxine (B6). They support a range of activities in the body including producing energy, supporting the nervous and immune systems, producing healthy skin, hair and nails, controlling feelings of stress and helping us to metabolize food properly. They can be found in fruit and vegetables including figs, dates, watermelons, apricots, bananas, berries, pineapples, oranges, cauliflowers, leeks, broccoli, spinach, watercress, beansprouts, peppers, avocados, celery, walnuts, barley, bulgur wheat, oats, milk and dairy products, eggs and prawns.

FOLIC ACID Part of the B vitamin group, this nutrient is essential before conception and during early pregnancy for the healthy development of the foetus. Good sources of folic acid include citrus fruits, broccoli, leafy green vegetables, beetroot, pumpkin, almonds, peanuts and lentils.

VITAMIN C Essential for supporting the immune system and bone health, vitamin C also aids skin repair and recuperation, assists with the absorption of iron and helps to protect against heart disease and cancer. Some good sources include citrus fruits, kiwi fruit, strawberries, blackcurrants, tomatoes and peppers.

VITAMIN E Found in leafy green vegetables, almonds, peanuts, pumpkin seeds, oats and eggs, this vitamin helps to thin the blood and protect against heart disease and ageing.

VITAMIN K Important for blood clotting, wound repair and healthy bones, vitamin K can be found in cauliflower, and kale, spinach and other leafy green vegetables.

CALCIUM Essential for healthy bones – so especially important for growing kids and women of menopausal age. Calcium also supports heart health, blood circulation, nerve impulse transmission and muscle function. It can be found in milk and dairy products, tofu, broccoli, leafy green vegetables, figs, almonds, sesame seeds and oats.

IRON It's essential that you get enough iron in your diet because it's important for making the haemoglobin that carries oxygen in the blood. Deficiency leads to lethargy and slowed mental function. You can find it in red meat, leafy green vegetables and dried fruit such as apricots, pumpkin seeds, sesame seeds, lentils, oats and prawns.

MAGNESIUM Like calcium, magnesium supports healthy bones and muscle function. It can be found in leafy green vegetables, citrus fruits and dried fruit, almonds, pumpkin seeds, sesame seeds and oats.

POTASSIUM Good for bones, teeth and healthy kidneys, potassium can be found in all fruit and vegetables – so tuck in!

ZINC This important mineral helps with growth, healing, reproduction, immunity and digestion. Good sources include beans and pulses as well as broccoli, cauliflower, carrots, raspberries, pumpkin seeds, sesame seeds, barley, oats, prawns and red meat.

ESSENTIAL FATTY ACIDS Essential for the proper functioning of the body, fatty acids help with cell development and formation, brain function and the nervous system, and help to regulate thyroid and adrenal activity. They help to regulate blood pressure, immune response and liver function, and help to break down blood cholesterol. They are also believed to help against cancer, heart attack and stroke. There are two key fatty acids that are needed for good health: omega-3 and omega-6. Good sources of omega-3 fatty acids include oily fish, tofu and soya beans, walnuts and flaxseeds (and their oils). Good sources of omega-6 fatty acids include many nuts and their oils, and poultry.

BREAKFASTS

●●●● TROPICAL FRUIT SMOOTHIE SERVES 1

80g/2¾oz pitted mango, roughly chopped

80g/2¾oz cored pineapple, roughly chopped

1 large kiwi fruit, roughly chopped

2 tbsp low-fat bio yogurt

150ml/5fl oz/scant ⅔ cup orange juice

Put the fruit, yogurt and orange juice in a blender and blend until smooth and creamy. Add a splash of water if the mixture is too thick, then pour into a large glass and serve immediately.

CREAMY BANANA, NECTARINE & STRAWBERRY SMOOTHIE SERVES 1

1 banana, broken into chunks
80g/2¾oz/½ cup strawberries, hulled
1 nectarine, peeled, pitted and roughly
   chopped
125ml/4fl oz/½ cup ice-cold milk

Put the fruit and milk in a blender and blend until smooth and creamy. Pour into a large glass and serve immediately.

SUPER VEGGIES SERVES 1

3 large carrots, scrubbed and roughly
   chopped
80g/2¾oz cherry tomatoes
generous dash of Tabasco sauce

Push the carrots through a juicer to make 150ml/5fl oz/ scant ⅔ cup juice. Pour the juice into a blender, add the tomatoes and blend until smooth. Pour into a large glass, stir in Tabasco to taste and serve immediately.

●● RASPBERRY & ORANGE JUICE   SERVES 1

80g/2¾oz/⅔ cup raspberries
150ml/5fl oz/scant ⅔ cup orange juice

Put the raspberries and orange juice in a blender and blend until smooth. If you prefer a seedless juice, strain through a sieve. Pour into a large glass and serve immediately.

●●●● BIG BREAKFAST BLEND   SERVES 1

3 dried apricots, chopped
1 peach, pitted and roughly chopped
80g/2¾oz/½ cup strawberries, hulled
150ml/5fl oz/scant ⅔ cup apple juice
2 tbsp Greek yogurt

Put the fruit, apple juice and yogurt in a blender and blend until smooth and creamy. Pour into a large glass and serve immediately.

SUMMER FRUIT SMOOTHIE   SERVES 1

80g/2¾oz/½ cup strawberries, hulled
80g/2¾oz/½ cup blueberries
80g/2¾oz/heaped ½ cup cherries, pitted
4 tbsp low-fat bio yogurt
80ml/2½fl oz/⅓ cup ice-cold milk

Put the fruit, yogurt and milk in a blender and blend until smooth and creamy. Pour into a large glass and serve immediately.

●●●● CREAMY FRESH FRUIT MUESLI SERVES 1

2 heaped tbsp rolled oats

3 tbsp milk

2 tbsp Greek yogurt

1 tbsp honey

¼ tsp ground cinnamon

1 heaped tbsp sultanas

1 apple

1 pear

150ml/5fl oz/scant ⅔ cup orange juice,
   to serve

Combine the oats, milk, yogurt, honey, cinnamon and sultanas and leave to soak for at least 20 minutes. Grate the apple and stir into the oat mixture. Peel and core the pear, cut into wedges and scatter over the muesli. Serve with a glass of orange juice.

DRIED CHERRY GRANOLA WITH FRESH FRUIT SERVES 1

40g/1½oz/⅓ cup granola
1 heaped tbsp dried cherries
1 orange, peel and pith removed
1 nectarine, pitted and cut into
   bite-sized pieces
low-fat bio yogurt or milk, to serve

Combine the granola and dried cherries in a dessert bowl. Working over the bowl to catch any juice, cut between the orange segment membranes to remove the flesh. Scatter the orange segments over the granola, squeezing over any juice from the membranes, then scatter the nectarine pieces on top. Serve with yogurt or milk.

FRUITY QUINOA & FIG PORRIDGE   SERVES 1

50g/1¾oz/¼ cup quinoa
150ml/5fl oz/scant ⅔ cup orange juice
3 dried figs, chopped
good pinch of ground cinnamon
pinch of salt
double cream or low-fat bio yogurt, to serve

Put the quinoa, orange juice, figs, cinnamon and salt in a pan. Bring to the boil, then reduce the heat, cover and simmer for 20 minutes until the liquid is absorbed. Remove the pan from heat and leave to stand, covered, for about 10 minutes. Stir, tip into a bowl and serve immediately with cream or yogurt for drizzling.

SPICED RICE PORRIDGE WITH SUMMER BERRY COMPOTE   SERVES 1

50g/1¾oz/¼ cup basmati rice
250ml/9fl oz/1 cup milk
1½ tsp sugar
2 cardamom pods, seeds removed
   and crushed
¼ tsp freshly grated nutmeg
1 heaped tbsp sultanas
80g/2¾oz/⅔ cup raspberries
80g/2¾oz/½ cup blueberries
80g/2¾oz/½ cup strawberries, hulled
   and cut into bite-sized pieces if large
¼ tsp icing sugar (optional)

Put the rice, milk, sugar, spices, sultanas and 125ml/4fl oz/½ cup water in a pan and bring to the boil. Reduce the heat and simmer gently for about 15 minutes until the porridge is thick and creamy, stirring frequently. Meanwhile, put half the berries in a blender and blend until smooth. Tip the purée into a fine-mesh sieve set over a bowl and push it through with a wooden spoon to remove the pips. Add icing sugar to taste, if necessary. Pour the sauce over the remaining berries and toss well. Tip the porridge into a bowl, spoon over the berry compote and serve immediately.

CREAMY DATE PORRIDGE WITH BAKED AUTUMN FRUITS SERVES 2

160g/5½oz plums, pitted
160g/5½oz fresh figs, halved
1 tbsp caster sugar
125g/4½oz/1¼ cups rolled oats
2 heaped tbsp chopped dried dates
300ml/10fl oz/1¼ cups milk

Preheat the oven to 190°C/375°F/Gas 5. Arrange the plums and figs in a baking dish, cut side up, and sprinkle with the sugar. Bake for about 25 minutes until bubbling and tender. About 5 minutes before the end of the cooking time, put the oats, dates, milk and 300ml/10fl oz/ 1¼ cups water in a pan and bring to the boil. Reduce the heat and simmer gently for about 5 minutes until thick and creamy, stirring frequently. Remove the fruit from the oven. Serve the porridge immediately with the fruit and any juices spooned over the top.

SIMPLE SEED MUESLI WITH NECTARINE & BLUEBERRIES SERVES 1

40g/1½oz/heaped ⅓ cup rolled oats

1 tbsp sunflower seeds

1 tbsp pumpkin seeds

1 tbsp dried blueberries

80ml/2½fl oz/⅓ cup low-fat bio yogurt

1 nectarine, pitted and sliced

Heat a frying pan, add the oats and seeds and dry-fry for about 5 minutes until the mixture is light brown and crisp, stirring constantly. Tip into a bowl and leave to cool. Stir in the dried blueberries, then top with the yogurt and nectarine slices and serve.

●●●● FRESH FRUIT COMPOTE SERVES 2

160g/5½oz pitted plums
160g/5½oz pitted apricots
2 heaped tbsp dried blueberries
300ml/10fl oz/1¼ cups orange juice
2 tsp caster sugar, plus extra to taste
1 slice fresh root ginger
1 clove
Greek yogurt, to serve

Put the fruit, orange juice, sugar, ginger and clove in a pan and bring to the boil. Reduce the heat and simmer gently for about 20 minutes until tender, stirring occasionally. Remove the ginger and clove and check the sweetness, adding a little more sugar to taste. Serve hot or cold with Greek yogurt. Alternatively, leave to cool, then blend and stir into the yogurt.

FRESH FRUIT SALAD SERVES 1

1 banana, sliced
1 apple, peeled, cored and sliced
   into wedges
80g/2¾oz/½ cup strawberries, hulled
   and halved, or quartered if large
3 tbsp orange juice

Put the fruit in a bowl and pour over the orange juice.
Toss to combine and serve.

TROPICAL FRUIT SALAD SERVES 1

juice of ¼ lime
80g/2¾oz deseeded papaya, sliced
1 large kiwi fruit, sliced
80g/2¾oz pitted lychees
2 tbsp pineapple juice

Squeeze the lime juice over the papaya, then combine
with the kiwi fruit and lychees. Drizzle with the pineapple
juice, toss to combine and serve.

CITRUS SALAD WITH DRIED DATES   SERVES 1

½ pink grapefruit, peel and pith removed
1 orange, peel and pith removed
2 clementines
1 tbsp chopped dried dates
1 tbsp toasted flaked almonds

Working over a bowl to catch the juices, cut between the grapefruit segment membranes with a sharp knife to remove the flesh. Put the flesh in the bowl and squeeze out any juice from the membranes. Repeat with the orange, pouring any reserved juice over the fruit. Slice the clementines and add to the orange and grapefruit. Scatter the dates and almonds over the top, toss to combine and serve.

CHERRY & LIME PANCAKES WITH BLUEBERRIES

SERVES 4

115g/4oz/scant 1 cup self-raising flour
2 tbsp caster sugar
1 egg, beaten
150ml/5fl oz/scant ⅔ cup milk
grated zest of 1 lime
50g/1¾ oz/scant ½ cup dried cherries
sunflower oil, for brushing

TO SERVE
320g/11oz/2 cups blueberries
clear honey
Greek yogurt

Heat a non-stick frying pan over a low heat. Meanwhile, combine the flour and sugar in a bowl and make a well in the middle. Combine the egg and milk, then pour about half of the mixture into the flour and stir to make a smooth batter. Beat in the remaining egg and milk mixture and fold in the lime zest and dried cherries. When the pan is very hot, brush very lightly with oil. Drop tablespoonfuls of batter into the pan and cook for 1–2 minutes until bubbles appear on the surface. Flip the pancakes over and cook for a further 30 seconds until golden underneath. Keep them warm while you make the rest of the pancakes in the same way. Serve with the blueberries, honey and Greek yogurt.

●● FRENCH TOAST WITH MAPLE-TOSSED PEACH & RASPBERRIES SERVES 1

1 peach, peeled, pitted and sliced
  into wedges
80g/2¾oz/⅔ cup raspberries
½–1 tbsp maple syrup
1 egg
1 tbsp milk
½ tsp caster sugar
2 slices of white bread or brioche
sunflower oil, for brushing
sifted icing sugar, for dusting

Put the peach and raspberries in a bowl, drizzle with the maple syrup and toss to combine. Beat together the egg, milk and sugar, then pour into a shallow dish. Place both slices of bread in the egg mixture and leave them to soak. Heat a non-stick frying pan and brush with oil. Carefully transfer the soaked bread to the pan and cook for about 2 minutes until golden. Flip the bread over and cook for a further 1–2 minutes until golden underneath. Transfer to a serving plate, dust with icing sugar and serve immediately with the fruit piled on top.

THE BIG GRILL   SERVES 1

1 large, flat mushroom

olive oil, for drizzling

1 tomato, halved

80g/2¾oz slender asparagus spears

2 bacon rashers

salt and freshly ground black pepper

150ml/5fl oz/scant ⅔ cup orange juice,
   to serve

Preheat the grill. Put the mushroom on the grill pan, drizzle with a little olive oil and season with salt and pepper, then grill for about 5 minutes. Arrange the tomato halves, asparagus and bacon around the mushroom. Drizzle the tomato and asparagus with oil and season, then grill for about 3 minutes. Turn the asparagus and bacon over and cook for a further 2–3 minutes until the vegetables are tender and the bacon crispy. Serve with a glass of orange juice.

●●● COURGETTE PANCAKES WITH PAN-FRIED MUSHROOMS

SERVES 4

320g/11oz courgettes, grated
½ tbsp dried dill
½ tsp freshly ground black pepper
2 eggs, separated
225g/8oz feta cheese, crumbled
75g/2½oz/scant ⅔ cup plain flour
sunflower oil, for brushing
25g/1oz butter
320g/11oz mushrooms, sliced
salt and freshly ground black pepper
4 x 150ml/5fl oz/scant ⅔ cup orange juice,
    to serve

Combine the courgettes, dill, pepper, egg yolks and feta, then stir in the flour. Whisk the egg whites until stiff, stir a spoonful into the courgette mixture to loosen it, then fold in the remaining whites. Heat a non-stick frying pan until very hot, then brush lightly with oil. Drop tablespoonfuls of the batter into the pan, spacing them apart, and cook for 2–3 minutes until golden underneath, then carefully flip the pancakes over and cook for a further 2–3 minutes. Keep them warm while you cook the remaining pancakes. Meanwhile, heat the butter in a pan and fry the mushrooms for about 10 minutes until tender and all the juices have evaporated. Season to taste with salt and pepper, pile them on top of the warm pancakes and serve with glasses of orange juice.

●● BEANS ON TOAST SERVES 4

2 shallots, finely chopped
2 tbsp olive oil
320g/11oz tomatoes, skinned and chopped
3 tbsp orange juice
1 tsp soft brown sugar
400g/14oz can cannellini or borlotti beans,
    drained and rinsed
4 slices of wholemeal bread
salt and freshly ground black pepper

Gently fry the shallots in the oil for 2–3 minutes. Add the tomatoes, orange juice and sugar and season with salt and pepper. Stir in the beans and cook very gently for about 10 minutes, stirring occasionally and adding a splash of water if the sauce becomes too dry. Preheat the grill. Just before the beans are ready, toast the wholemeal bread. Check the beans' seasoning, then pile them on top of the slices of toast and serve immediately.

SMOKED MACKEREL & PEA KEDGEREE SERVES 4

200g/7oz/1 cup basmati rice

1 tsp turmeric

1 tsp ground cumin

2 tbsp olive oil

1 onion, finely chopped

2 red peppers, deseeded and sliced

280g/10oz smoked mackerel, skinned and
broken into large flakes

320g/11oz/2 cups frozen peas, thawed

80g/2¾oz/⅔ cup sultanas

salt and freshly ground black pepper

TO SERVE

lemon wedges

4 x 150ml/5fl oz/scant ⅔ cup apple juice

Put the rice in a pan with the spices and a pinch of salt, add 600ml/1 pint/2½ cups boiling water and bring to the boil. Reduce the heat, cover and simmer gently for 10 minutes until all the water has been absorbed. Meanwhile, heat the oil in a frying pan and fry the onion gently for 4 minutes, then add the peppers and fry for a further 5 minutes. Remove the rice from the heat, quickly add the mackerel and replace the lid, then leave to stand for 5 minutes. Add the peas and sultanas to the vegetables and warm through. Add the vegetables to the rice and fish, season with pepper and toss to combine. Serve with lemon wedges for squeezing over a glass of apple juice.

EGGS FLORENTINE ON MUFFINS   SERVES 2

15g/½oz butter
160g/5½oz spinach, tough stalks discarded
2 eggs
2–3 tbsp Hollandaise sauce
2 muffins, split in half
salt and freshly ground black pepper
2 x 150ml/5fl oz/scant ⅔ cup fruit juice,
   to serve

Melt the butter in a pan, then sauté the spinach for 2–3 minutes until it has wilted. Season to taste with salt and pepper and keep it warm. Half-fill a pan with water and bring to the boil, then reduce the heat to a bare simmer. Preheat the grill. One at a time, crack the eggs into a cup and slide them into the water. Poach for about 4 minutes, then remove with a slotted spoon and drain on kitchen paper. Meanwhile, toast the muffin halves under the hot grill. Place 2 muffin halves on each plate, top with some spinach, then an egg, and spoon the Hollandaise sauce over the top. Give a final grinding of pepper, then serve with a glass of fruit juice.

SCRAMBLED EGGS WITH TOMATOES & PEPPERS

SERVES 2

1 tbsp olive oil
1 red pepper, deseeded and diced
4 eggs
good pinch of thyme leaves
160g/5½oz tomatoes, deseeded and
   chopped
salt and freshly ground black pepper

TO SERVE
wholemeal toast (optional)
2 x 150ml/5fl oz/scant ⅔ cup orange juice

Heat the oil in a non-stick frying pan and gently fry the peppers for about 5 minutes. Meanwhile, beat the eggs and season with salt and pepper. Pour them into the pan, add the thyme and cook very gently until the eggs are creamy but not set, stirring constantly. Add the tomatoes and continue cooking until the eggs are set to your liking and the tomatoes are warmed through. Serve with toast, if using, a glass of orange juice.

LIGHT MEALS

●●● THAI-SPICED BROCCOLI, SPINACH & CAULIFLOWER SOUP   SERVES 4

3 garlic cloves, crushed
2 tsp grated fresh root ginger
2 tsp Thai green curry paste
2 tbsp sunflower oil
1.25 litres/2 pints/5 cups vegetable stock
320g/11oz broccoli, cut into small florets
320g/11oz cauliflower, cut into small florets
320g/11oz spinach, tough stalks discarded
4 tbsp creamed coconut
salt and freshly ground black pepper
sliced red chillies, to scatter

Gently fry the garlic, ginger and green curry paste in the oil for about 1 minute. Add the stock, broccoli and cauliflower, and bring to the boil. Reduce the heat, cover and simmer for about 5 minutes until the vegetables are tender. Remove about half the broccoli and cauliflower from the pan using a slotted spoon and set aside. Add the spinach to the pan and cook for about 1 minute until wilted. Pour the contents of the pan into a food processor or blender and processs until smooth. Return the soup to the pan, stir in the creamed coconut and reserved cauliflower and broccoli, season to taste with salt and pepper and warm through. Serve scattered with sliced red chillies.

●●●● CHUNKY LENTIL & COCONUT SOUP   SERVES 4

2 tbsp sunflower oil
3 garlic cloves, crushed
¼ tsp crushed dried chillies
2 tsp ground cumin
1 tsp turmeric
½ tsp ground cinnamon
1.25 litres/2 pints/5 cups vegetable stock
115g/4oz/scant ½ cup red lentils
320g/11oz celery, sliced
320g/11oz carrots, diced
320g/11oz peeled and cored apples, diced
4 tbsp coconut cream
juice of ½ lime
salt and freshly ground black pepper
handful of coriander leaves, to scatter

Heat the oil in a pan and gently fry the garlic for about 1 minute. Stir in the spices, then add the stock, lentils, celery, carrots and apple. Bring to the boil, then reduce the heat, cover and simmer for about 30 minutes until the lentils are tender. Stir in the coconut cream and lime juice to taste and season with salt and pepper. Serve scattered with coriander leaves.

●● CREAMY PEA & BROAD BEAN SOUP SERVES 4

3 shallots, finely chopped

2 garlic cloves, crushed

2 tbsp olive oil

450g/1lb/3 cups frozen peas

450g/1lb/2½ cups frozen broad beans

1.25 litres/2 pints/5 cups vegetable or
   chicken stock

80ml/2½fl oz/⅓ cup double cream

salt and freshly ground black pepper

mint leaves, to scatter

Gently fry the shallots and garlic in the oil for about 2 minutes. Add the peas, beans and stock and bring to the boil. Pour the contents of the pan into a food processor or blender and processs until smooth. Return to the pan, season to taste with salt and pepper and heat through. Swirl some cream through each serving and scatter with mint leaves.

ITALIAN BEAN & CABBAGE SOUP SERVES 4

320g/11oz onions, finely chopped

3 garlic cloves, crushed

2 tbsp olive oil

400g/14oz can chopped tomatoes

1 tbsp tomato purée

1.25 litres/2 pints/5 cups vegetable stock

400g/14oz can cannellini beans, drained
  and rinsed

320g/11oz cabbage, shredded

salt and freshly ground black pepper

Parmesan cheese shavings, to scatter

Gently fry the onions and garlic in the oil for 4 minutes. Add the tomatoes, purée and stock and bring to the boil. Reduce the heat, cover and simmer for about 20 minutes. Put a quarter of the beans and a couple of ladlefuls of soup into a food processor or blender and process until smooth, then stir back into the soup. Return to a simmer, stir in the cabbage and remaining beans and simmer for 5–10 minutes until the cabbage is tender. Season to taste with salt and pepper, and serve with Parmesan shavings to scatter.

● ● ● CREAMY CARROT, LEEK & TOMATO SOUP   SERVES 4

320g/11oz leeks, sliced
2 tbsp olive oil
320g/11oz carrots, sliced
320g/11oz tomatoes, skinned and chopped
1.25 litres/2 pints/5 cups vegetable stock
2 tbsp double cream
salt and freshly ground black pepper

Gently fry the leeks in the oil for about 5 minutes. Add the carrots, tomatoes and stock and bring to the boil. Reduce the heat, cover and simmer for about 20 minutes until the vegetables are tender. Pour the soup into a food processor or blender and processs until smooth. Return to the pan, stir in the cream, season to taste with salt and pepper and warm through.

● ● SIMPLE VEGETABLE MINESTRONE   SERVES 4

1 onion, finely chopped
2 garlic cloves, crushed
2 tbsp olive oil
400g/14oz can chopped tomatoes
1.25 litres/2 pints/5 cups vegetable stock
320g/11oz courgettes, quartered
    lengthways and thinly sliced
80g/2¾oz vermicelli, broken into short
    lengths, or soup pasta
2 tbsp pesto
salt and freshly ground black pepper
Parmesan cheese shavings, to scatter

Gently fry the onion and garlic in the oil for 4 minutes. Add the tomatoes and stock and bring to the boil. Reduce the heat, cover and simmer gently for 15 minutes. Add the courgettes and simmer for 5 minutes, then add the pasta and cook for 2–4 minutes until the pasta and courgettes are tender. Stir in the pesto, season to taste with salt and pepper and serve scattered with Parmesan shavings.

CHARGRILLED CHICKEN SALAD SERVES 4

2 handfuls of salad leaves
2 yellow peppers, deseeded and diced
320g/11oz drained bottled or canned
   artichokes, cut into quarters
320g/11oz cherry tomatoes, halved
320g/11oz kiwi fruits, cut into bite-sized
   pieces
2 chargrilled chicken breasts, sliced

FOR THE DRESSING
1 tbsp white wine vinegar
2½ tbsp olive oil
¼ tsp grated unwaxed lemon zest
1 tsp Dijon mustard
pinch of sugar
freshly ground black pepper

To make the dressing, whisk together the vinegar, oil, lemon zest, mustard, sugar and pepper to taste. Arrange the salad leaves on 4 plates and scatter the peppers, artichokes, tomatoes, kiwi fruits and chicken over them. Drizzle the dressing over the top, toss lightly to combine and serve.

CHICKEN, GREEN PEPPER & MANGO WRAPS SERVES 2

1 chargrilled chicken breast, cut into
   bite-sized pieces
1 green pepper, deseeded and diced
160g/5½oz pitted mango, diced
2 tortilla wraps

FOR THE DRESSING
1 tbsp olive oil
1 tsp red wine vinegar
½ tsp Dijon mustard
good pinch of crushed dried chillies
pinch of sugar

To make the dressing, whisk together the oil, vinegar, mustard, dried chillies and sugar. Mix together the chicken, pepper and mango, spoon the dressing over the top and toss to combine. Lay the tortilla wraps on a board and spread half the filling down the centre of each one. Fold the bottom end over the filling, then roll up each wrap and serve.

CHICKEN PITTA POCKETS WITH GINGERY CARROT & BEANSPROUT SALAD SERVES 4

320g/11oz carrots, grated
320g/11oz/3½ cups beansprouts
2 spring onions, thinly sliced
4 pitta breads
2 roast chicken breasts, sliced

FOR THE DRESSING
2 tsp grated fresh root ginger
1 tbsp sweet chilli sauce
2 tsp white wine vinegar
2 tbsp sunflower oil
salt

To make the dressing, whisk together the ginger, chilli sauce, vinegar and oil and season to taste with salt. Combine the carrots, beansprouts and spring onions, drizzle with the dressing and toss well. Warm the pitta breads under a preheated grill or in a toaster, then split open and divide the chicken between them. Pile the carrot and beansprout salad on top and serve with any extra on the side.

●●●● CHICKEN SATAY SALAD   SERVES 4

1 garlic clove, crushed

1 tsp grated fresh root ginger

1 tbsp olive oil

2 skinless, boneless chicken breasts, each
    sliced into 6–8 long strips

320g/11oz carrots, cut into matchsticks

320g/11oz/3½ cups beansprouts

320g/11oz cucumber, halved lengthways
    and sliced

2 yellow peppers, deseeded and sliced

large handful of coriander leaves

FOR THE DRESSING

1 tbsp peanut butter

¼ tsp crushed dried chillies

4 tsp white wine vinegar

3 tbsp sunflower oil

1 tsp sesame oil

½–1 tsp soy sauce

Soak 12–16 bamboo skewers in water for 20 minutes.
Whisk together the garlic, ginger and oil, pour over the
chicken and toss to combine. Cover and marinate in the
fridge for at least 30 minutes. To make the dressing, whisk
all the ingredients together, adding soy sauce to taste.
Toss together the carrots, beansprouts, cucumber, peppers
and coriander. Divide among 4 plates and drizzle with the
dressing. Meanwhile, thread the chicken on to the skewers
and cook under a preheated grill for about 3 minutes
on each side until cooked through. Place on top of the
dressed salads and serve.

SMOKED CHICKEN SANDWICHES SERVES 2

1 avocado, pitted

4 slices of Granary bread

1 smoked chicken breast, sliced

2 tomatoes, deseeded and chopped

2 tsp sweet chilli sauce

3–4 large basil leaves, torn

¼ lime

2 dessert bowls of salad, to serve

Scoop the avocado flesh into a bowl, mash roughly with a fork, then spread over 2 slices of the bread. Top with the smoked chicken and tomatoes, then drizzle with chilli sauce. Scatter the basil leaves on top, squeeze some lime juice over each sandwich base, then top with the remaining bread slices. Cut in half, arrange on plates and serve the sandwiches with side salads.

●●● CHICKEN WALDORF SALAD   SERVES 4

2 cooked chicken breasts, cut into
   bite-sized pieces
320g/11oz peeled, cored apples, cut
   into bite-sized pieces
320g/11oz celery, chopped
80g/2¾oz/½ cup walnuts
4 heaped tbsp sultanas
chopped parsley, to scatter

FOR THE DRESSING
125ml/4fl oz/½ cup mayonnaise
½ tsp unwaxed grated lemon zest
1 tsp lemon juice
freshly ground black pepper

To make the dressing, whisk together the mayonnaise, lemon zest and juice and season with black pepper. Mix together the chicken, apples, celery, walnuts and sultanas, spoon the dressing on top and toss to combine. Scatter with chopped parsley and serve.

VEGETABLE & LAMB SKEWERS WITH WATERMELON SALAD SERVES 4

2 garlic cloves, crushed

2 tsp ground cumin

2 tsp paprika

2 tbsp olive oil

450g/1lb boneless shoulder of lamb, cut into large cubes

2 red onions, cut into eighths

2 red peppers, deseeded and cut into eighths

salt and freshly ground black pepper

FOR THE SALAD

320g/11oz deseeded watermelon, cut into bite-sized chunks

320g/11oz deseeded cucumber, finely diced

handful of black olives

2 tbsp toasted pine nuts

2 tbsp olive oil

2½ tsp white wine vinegar

Whisk together the garlic, cumin, paprika and oil and season well with salt and pepper. Pour the mixture over the lamb, cover and marinate in the fridge for at least 2 hours. Preheat the grill to high. Thread alternating pieces of onion, pepper and lamb on to 8 metal skewers and grill for 4–5 minutes on each side or until the lamb is cooked to your liking. Meanwhile, to make the salad, mix together the watermelon, cucumber, olives and pine nuts in a bowl. Season to taste, sprinkle the oil and vinegar over the top and toss to combine. Serve with the skewers.

●●● LAMB KOFTA WITH SPICY TOMATO CITRUS SALAD   SERVES 4

450g/1lb lean minced lamb
1 tsp paprika
1 tsp ground cumin
2 garlic cloves, crushed
grated zest and juice of 1 unwaxed lemon
½ onion, grated
salt and freshly ground black pepper

FOR THE SALAD
4 oranges, peel and pith removed
320g/11oz deseeded cucumber, diced
320g/11oz deseeded tomatoes, chopped
handful of basil leaves, torn (optional)

FOR THE DRESSING
2½ tsp red wine vinegar

good pinch of sugar
2 green chillies, deseeded and chopped
2 tbsp olive oil

Mix together the lamb, spices, garlic, lemon zest and juice and onion and season well with salt and pepper. Mould into 8 egg-shaped pieces, then thread on to 8 metal skewers. Cover and refrigerate for at least 30 minutes. Meanwhile, to make the salad, cut between the orange segment membranes to remove the flesh, then mix it in a bowl with the cucumber and tomatoes. Whisk together the dressing ingredients and season with salt. Drizzle it over the salad and toss to combine. Preheat the grill and cook the lamb for about 8 minutes until cooked through, turning occasionally. Serve with the salad.

●● GRILLED CHOPS WITH GREEN BEAN & COURGETTE SALAD   SERVES 4

½ garlic clove, crushed
½ tsp paprika
1 tbsp olive oil
4 lamb chops
salt and freshly ground black pepper

FOR THE DRESSING
2½ tsp cider vinegar
2 tbsp olive oil
1 tsp Dijon mustard
good pinch of sugar
¼ tsp grated lemon zest

FOR THE SALAD
320g/11oz trimmed green beans
320g/11oz courgettes, cut into batons

Combine the garlic, paprika and oil and season with salt and pepper. Pour the mixture over the lamb chops to coat, cover and marinate in the fridge for at least 30 minutes. To make the dressing, whisk together the vinegar, oil, mustard, sugar and lemon zest and season to taste with salt and pepper. Cook the beans in boiling water for 3–4 minutes until just tender, then drain and refresh under cold water. Steam the courgettes over a pan of simmering water for about 2 minutes until just tender, then put in a bowl with the beans, drizzle with the dressing and toss to combine. Meanwhile, preheat the grill and cook the chops for about 3 minutes on each side. Serve the chops with the salad.

MARINATED LAMB & KIWI SALAD SERVES 4

1 tbsp olive oil

1 tbsp lemon juice

1 tbsp chopped oregano

2 lamb steaks

320g/11oz sugar snap peas

2 handfuls of salad leaves

2 green peppers, deseeded and cut into
  bite-sized pieces

4 large kiwi fruit, halved and sliced

320g/11oz cherry tomatoes, halved

salt and freshly ground black pepper

FOR THE DRESSING

1 tbsp red wine vinegar

½ tsp ground cumin

good pinch of sugar

2½ tbsp olive oil

Whisk together the oil, lemon juice and oregano and season well with salt and pepper. Pour the mixture over the lamb steaks, cover and marinate in the fridge for at least 2 hours. Cook the sugar snap peas in boiling water for about 3 minutes until just tender, then drain and refresh under cold water. Put the salad leaves in a serving bowl and scatter the peppers, kiwis, tomatoes and sugar snap peas on top. To make the dressing, whisk together the vinegar, cumin, sugar and oil and season to taste. Preheat the grill and cook the lamb steaks for 2–3 minutes on each side until cooked to your liking. Slice the lamb and add to the salad. Drizzle with the dressing and serve immediately.

●●● LAMB CUTLETS WITH GARLIC SPINACH SERVES 4

2 garlic cloves, crushed
1 tsp ground coriander
juice of ½ lemon
1 tbsp olive oil
8 lamb cutlets
salt and freshly ground black pepper

FOR THE GARLIC SPINACH
2 tbsp olive oil
2 tbsp pine nuts
2 garlic cloves, crushed
320g/11oz tomatoes, skinned and chopped
4 heaped tbsp sultanas
320g/11oz spinach, tough stalks discarded

Whisk together the garlic, coriander, lemon juice and oil and season well with salt and pepper. Pour the mixture over the cutlets, cover and marinate in the fridge for at least 1 hour. To make the garlic spinach, heat the oil in a frying pan and fry the pine nuts for 3–4 minutes until golden, stirring frequently. Add the garlic and fry for 1 minute, then add the tomatoes and sultanas and cook gently for about 5 minutes. Toss in the spinach and cook for about 2 minutes until wilted. Season to taste with salt and pepper. Meanwhile, preheat the grill and cook the cutlets for 3–4 minutes on each side until cooked to your liking, then serve on a bed of spinach.

●● MARINATED LAMB SKEWERS WITH CUCUMBER & PEPPER SALAD SERVES 4

2 garlic cloves, crushed
1 tsp chopped rosemary
2 tsp paprika
juice of ½ lemon
2 tbsp olive oil
500g/1lb 2oz boneless shoulder of lamb, cubed
2 yellow peppers, deseeded and chopped
320g/11oz deseeded cucumber, diced
handful of parsley, chopped
salt and freshly ground black pepper

FOR THE DRESSING
2½ tsp red wine vinegar
2 tbsp olive oil
good pinch of crushed dried chillies

Soak 8–12 bamboo skewers in water for 20 minutes. Whisk together the garlic, rosemary, paprika, lemon juice and oil and season well. Pour the mixture over the lamb, cover and marinate in the fridge for at least 1 hour. Preheat the grill, thread the lamb on to the skewers and grill for 4–5 minutes on each side until cooked to your liking. Meanwhile, mix the peppers and cucumber in a bowl and scatter with the parsley. To make the dressing, whisk together the vinegar, oil and dried chillies and season to taste with salt. Drizzle over the salad, toss to combine, then serve with the lamb skewers.

●●●● WARM RICE SALAD WITH SPICY SAUSAGE   SERVES 4

200g/7oz/1 cup basmati rice

320g/11oz green beans, trimmed and cut
   into 3cm/1½in lengths

320g/11oz/heaped 1½ cups drained
   canned sweetcorn

2 red peppers, deseeded and diced

12 dried apricots, diced

80g/2¾oz chorizo, diced

large handful of flat-leaf parsley, chopped

salt

FOR THE DRESSING

1 tsp Dijon mustard

good pinch of crushed dried chillies

2 tsp red wine vinegar

2 tbsp olive oil

Put the rice in a pan with 600ml/21fl oz/2½ cups boiling water and a pinch of salt. Bring to the boil, then reduce the heat, cover and simmer for 10 minutes. Remove from the heat and leave to stand for 5 minutes. Meanwhile, cook the beans in boiling water for 3–4 minutes until just tender, then drain and refresh under cold water. Fluff up the rice with a fork and add the beans, corn, peppers, apricots and chorizo. To make the dressing, whisk together the mustard, dried chillies, vinegar and oil and pour over the salad. Add the parsley and toss the mixture well, then check the seasoning and serve.

RICE NOODLE SALAD WITH PORK SERVES 4

115g/4oz rice noodles
2 tbsp sunflower oil
3 garlic cloves, crushed
2 tsp grated fresh root ginger
2 green chillies, deseeded and finely
  chopped
400g/14oz minced pork
½ tsp five spice powder
2 tsp soy sauce
2 tsp rice wine
320g/11oz tomatoes, cut into eighths
2 green peppers, deseeded and thinly sliced
320g/11oz/3½ cups beansprouts
handful of watercress

FOR THE DRESSING
2 tbsp sunflower oil

1 tsp sesame oil
2 tsp soy sauce
2 tsp grated fresh root ginger
2 tsp sweet chilli sauce
2 tsp white wine vinegar

Soak the noodles in boiling water for 5 minutes until tender, then drain well and set aside. Heat the oil in a frying pan and gently fry the garlic, ginger and chillies for about 1 minute. Add the pork and five spice powder and stir-fry for about 2 minutes. Add the soy sauce and rice wine and cook for 2 minutes. To make the dressing, whisk together the oils, soy sauce, ginger, chilli sauce and vinegar. Snip the noodles into 5cm/2in lengths and toss with the tomatoes, peppers, beansprouts, watercress and pork mixture. Drizzle with the dressing, toss to combine and serve.

BORLOTTI BEAN & BACON SALAD WITH ARTICHOKES, GREEN BEANS & CHERRY TOMATOES SERVES 4

320g/11oz trimmed green beans, cut into
3cm/1½in lengths
2 x 400g/14oz cans borlotti beans, drained
and rinsed
320g/11oz cherry tomatoes, halved
320g/11oz drained canned or bottled
artichokes, quartered
4 bacon rashers, grilled

FOR THE DRESSING
2 tsp sun-dried tomato pesto
1 tbsp red wine vinegar
2½ tbsp olive oil
freshly ground black pepper

Cook the green beans in boiling water for 4 minutes until just tender, then drain and refresh under cold water. Put them in a serving bowl with the borlotti beans, tomatoes and artichokes. To make the dressing, whisk together the pesto, vinegar and oil and season to taste with pepper. Drizzle the dressing over the vegetables. Snip the grilled bacon into bite-sized pieces and scatter over the salad, then toss to combine and serve.

PROSCIUTTO, PEACH & RED ONION SALAD SERVES 4

320g/11oz red onions, cut into wedges
1 tbsp olive oil
2 handfuls of salad leaves
4 ripe peaches, pitted and cut into
large wedges
8 slices of prosciutto, torn into bite-sized
pieces
freshly ground black pepper

FOR THE DRESSING
1½ tbsp balsamic vinegar
1 tbsp olive oil
1 tsp wholegrain mustard

Preheat the oven to 190°C/375°F/Gas 5. Put the onions in a baking dish, drizzle over the oil, season with pepper and roast in the hot oven for about 15 minutes until just tender. Meanwhile, divide the salad leaves between 4 plates, then scatter the peach wedges and prosciutto over the top. To make the dressing, whisk together the vinegar, oil and mustard. Scatter the roasted onions over the salad and drizzle with the dressing, then grind over some pepper and serve.

●● TOASTED AVOCADO BLT   SERVES 1

2 slices of bread
3 bacon rashers
1 tbsp mayonnaise
½ avocado, pitted and sliced
1 tomato, sliced
2–3 crisp lettuce leaves
freshly ground black pepper

Preheat the grill to high, then toast the bread on both sides and grill the bacon until crisp. Spread each slice of toast with the mayonnaise, top one slice with avocado and tomato and grind over a little pepper. Top with the bacon and lettuce and finish with the second slice of toast. Serve immediately.

●●● PORK SKEWERS WITH GRAPEFRUIT SALAD   SERVES 4

300g/10½oz minced pork
2 tsp grated fresh root ginger
2 green chillies, deseeded and finely
  chopped
2 garlic cloves, crushed
2 tsp soy sauce
handful of coriander leaves, chopped
8 lemongrass stalks
2 pink grapefruit, peel and pith removed
2 avocados
1 large handful of watercress
1 large handful of rocket
320g/11oz/3½ cups beansprouts

FOR THE DRESSING
2½ tsp white wine vinegar
2 tbsp olive oil

pinch of sugar
salt and freshly ground black pepper

Put the pork, ginger, chillies, garlic, soy sauce and coriander in a bowl and mix thoroughly. Form into 8 egg-shaped pieces and thread on to the lemongrass stalks. Cover and chill for 30 minutes. Preheat the grill and cook the skewers for about 3 minutes on each side until cooked through. Meanwhile, cut between the grapefruit segment membranes with a sharp knife to remove the flesh. Halve, pit and peel the avocados, then slice the flesh. Divide the watercress and rocket between 4 plates and scatter over the beansprouts, grapefruit and avocados. To make the dressing, whisk together the vinegar, oil and sugar, season to taste and drizzle it over the salad. Place the pork skewers on top and serve.

SEARED BEEF SALAD SERVES 4

250g/9oz beef sirloin

olive oil, for brushing

320g/11oz mangetouts

2 large handfuls of mixed salad leaves

320g/11oz pitted mango, diced

320g/11oz cucumber, thinly sliced

2 yellow peppers, deseeded and sliced

FOR THE DRESSING

1 tbsp white wine vinegar

1 tsp wasabi paste

2½ tbsp sunflower oil

salt and freshly ground black pepper

Brush the beef with oil. Heat a griddle pan until very hot, then sear the meat for about 2 minutes on each side until cooked to your liking. Remove from the heat and leave to rest for about 10 minutes. Meanwhile, cook the mangetouts in a pan of boiling water for about 3 minutes until just tender, then refresh under cold water and drain well. Divide the salad leaves among 4 plates, then scatter the mango, cucumber, peppers and mangetouts over the top. To make the dressing, whisk together the vinegar, wasabi and oil and season to taste with salt and pepper. Slice the beef thinly, pile it on top of the salad and drizzle with the dressing. Serve immediately.

●●●● BEEF PATTIES WITH ROASTED VEGETABLE WEDGES

SERVES 4

2 red onions, cut into large wedges

320g/11oz deseeded butternut squash,
cut into chunks

320g/11oz beetroot, cut into wedges

2 tbsp olive oil

1 tsp thyme leaves

1½ tsp balsamic vinegar

450g/1lb minced beef

1 small onion, grated

2 garlic cloves, crushed

¼ tsp crushed dried chillies

1 tsp tomato ketchup, plus extra to serve

1 egg, beaten

salt and freshly ground black pepper

4 dessert bowls of salad, to serve

Preheat the oven to 190°C/375°F/Gas 5. Put the onions, squash and beetroot in a baking dish. Whisk together the oil, thyme and vinegar and season with salt and pepper. Drizzle the mixture over the vegetables, then toss to coat. Roast in the hot oven for about 25 minutes until tender, turning once or twice. Meanwhile, mix together the beef, onion, garlic, chillies, ketchup and egg and season with salt and pepper. Shape the mixture into 4 patties. About 10 minutes before the vegetables are cooked, preheat the grill and cook the patties for 5–6 minutes on each side until browned and cooked through. Put a patty and some vegetable wedges on each plate and serve with a side salad and some ketchup.

PASTRAMI ON RYE WITH CARROT & CABBAGE COLESLAW SERVES 2

¼–½ tsp Dijon mustard
4 slices of rye bread
4 thin slices of pastrami
4 slices of Swiss cheese
sweet dill pickles, to serve

FOR THE COLESLAW
160g/5½oz white cabbage, shredded
2 carrots, grated
2 heaped tbsp raisins
3 tbsp mayonnaise
2 tbsp low-fat bio yogurt
freshly ground black pepper

To make the coleslaw, mix together the cabbage, carrots and raisins in a bowl. Stir the mayonnaise and yogurt together, then fold into the vegetables. Season with pepper and set aside. Spread a thin layer of mustard on 2 slices of the bread and top each one with 2 slices of pastrami and 2 slices of Swiss cheese. Top each sandwich with the second slice of rye bread and serve the sandwiches and coleslaw with the dill pickles.

●● BEEF BAGUETTES WITH SWEET PEPPER & HORSERADISH RELISH   SERVES 2

250g/9oz beef sirloin
olive oil, for brushing
2 small baguettes
160g/5½oz cucumber, sliced lengthways

FOR THE RELISH
1½ tbsp olive oil
1 garlic clove, crushed
1 red pepper, deseeded and chopped
½ tsp grated horseradish
salt

To make the relish, heat the oil in a frying pan and gently fry the garlic for about 1 minute. Add the pepper and cook gently for about 15 minutes, stirring occasionally. Tip the mixture into a food processor, add the horseradish and process until coarsely chopped. Season to taste with salt and set aside. Brush the beef with oil. Heat a griddle pan until very hot, then cook the meat for about 2 minutes on each side until cooked to your liking. Remove from the heat and leave to rest for about 10 minutes, then slice thinly. Split the baguettes in half, fill with the beef, cucumber and relish and serve immediately.

●● BAKED POTATOES TOPPED WITH CHILLI BEEF   SERVES 4

4 large potatoes
1 tbsp olive oil, plus extra for rubbing
2 garlic cloves, crushed
350g/12oz minced beef
320g/11oz tomatoes, skinned and chopped
1 tbsp tomato purée
100ml/3½fl oz/scant ½ cup beef stock
400g/14oz can kidney beans, drained
   and rinsed
1 tsp ground cumin
¼–½ tsp crushed dried chillies
4 tbsp sour cream
salt and freshly ground black pepper
shredded spring onion, to scatter

Preheat the oven to 190°C/375°F/Gas 5. Prick the potatoes all over, rub with oil and bake in the hot oven for 1–1½ hours until cooked. Meanwhile, heat the oil in a pan and fry the garlic for 1 minute, then add the beef and fry gently until browned. Add the tomatoes, tomato purée, stock, beans and spices and season with salt and pepper. Simmer for 15–20 minutes, stirring occasionally, then check the seasoning. Cut the potatoes open and spoon the chilli beef over the top. Add a dollop of sour cream, scatter with some shredded spring onions and serve.

● ● ● CHILLI TOMATO BEEF & AVOCADO WRAPS   SERVES 4

1 tbsp olive oil

2 garlic cloves, crushed

225g/8oz minced beef

320g/11oz tomatoes, skinned and chopped

1 tbsp tomato purée

1 tsp ground cumin

½ tsp crushed dried chillies

4 heaped tbsp canned kidney beans,
   drained and rinsed

2 avocados

4 flour tortillas

handful of coriander leaves

salt and freshly ground black pepper

TO SERVE

4 tbsp sour cream

4 dessert bowls of salad

Heat the oil in a large frying pan and fry the garlic for about 1 minute, then add the beef and fry gently until browned all over. Add the tomatoes, tomato purée, spices and beans and season with salt and pepper. Simmer for 15–20 minutes, stirring occasionally, then check the seasoning. Just before the beef is ready, halve, pit and peel the avocados and dice the flesh. Fold the tortillas into cones, then spoon some of the chilli beef into each one. Top with avocado and coriander and serve with sour cream and side salads.

SALAD NIÇOISE SERVES 4

350g/12oz new potatoes, halved if large

320g/11oz trimmed green beans

2 tuna steaks (about 150g/5½oz each)

olive oil, for brushing

2 Baby Gem lettuces, leaves torn into
  bite-sized pieces

320g/11oz cherry tomatoes, halved

2 yellow peppers, deseeded and cut into
  bite-sized chunks

320g/11oz deseeded cucumber, halved
  lengthways and sliced

80g/2¾oz black olives

4 hard-boiled eggs, cut into quarters

salt and freshly ground black pepper

FOR THE DRESSING

½ garlic clove, crushed

1 tsp Dijon mustard

good pinch of sugar

1½ tbsp red wine vinegar

3 tbsp olive oil

Boil the potatoes for about 10 minutes until tender, then drain. Boil the beans for 3–4 minutes until just tender and refresh under cold water. Meanwhile, whisk together the dressing ingredients and season to taste with salt and pepper. Brush the tuna with oil and season with salt and pepper. Heat a griddle pan until very hot, then cook the tuna for 1–2 minutes on each side until cooked but still pink in the middle. Divide the lettuce leaves, vegetables and olives between 4 plates. Drizzle with the dressing and toss lightly. Slice the tuna thickly, arrange on top of the salads with the eggs and serve.

ZINGY PRAWN SALAD SERVES 4

115g/4oz mixed salad leaves
320g/11oz cucumber, halved lengthways
   and thinly sliced
320g/11oz pitted mango, diced
2 avocados, pitted and diced
320g/11oz/3½ cups beansprouts
250g/9oz cooked, peeled tiger prawns
handful of basil leaves, torn (optional)

FOR THE DRESSING
grated zest and juice of 1 lime
2 tsp sweet chilli sauce
2 tbsp sunflower oil
salt

To make the dressing, whisk together the lime zest and juice, sweet chilli sauce and oil and season to taste with salt. Divide the salad leaves between 4 bowls, scatter the cucumber, mango, avocados, beansprouts and prawns on top, then sprinkle the basil leaves over, if using. Drizzle with the dressing, toss lightly to combine and serve.

CRAB CAKES WITH SPICY MANGO SALSA SERVES 4

2 x 175g/6oz cans crab meat
1 tbsp green curry paste
1 tsp Thai fish sauce
2 tbsp plain flour
1 egg, beaten
sunflower oil, for frying
4 large handfuls of rocket

FOR THE SALSA
320g/11oz pitted mango, diced
1 red chilli, deseeded and finely chopped
handful of coriander leaves, finely chopped
juice of 1 lime
salt

To make the salsa, put the mango, chilli and coriander leaves in a bowl, squeeze over the lime juice, add a pinch of salt and toss well. In a separate bowl, combine the crab meat, curry paste and fish sauce. Add the flour and egg and mix well. Shape the mixture into 12 small cakes. Heat some oil in a frying pan and fry the cakes for 3–4 minutes on each side until golden. Drain on kitchen paper. Serve the crab cakes and the salsa with the rocket.

● ● ● TABBOULEH WITH SMOKED TROUT & ROASTED SQUASH SERVES 4

320g/11oz deseeded butternut squash,
  cut into chunks
3 tbsp olive oil
200g/7oz/heaped 1 cup bulgur wheat
320g/11oz cherry tomatoes, halved
320g/11oz deseeded cucumber, diced
handful of parsley, chopped
handful of mint, chopped
juice of 1 lemon
175g/6oz smoked trout fillets, flaked
salt and freshly ground black pepper

Preheat the oven to 200°C/400°F/Gas 6. Put the squash in a baking dish, drizzle with 1 tbsp of the oil, season with salt and pepper and toss to coat. Roast in the hot oven for about 25 minutes until tender. Meanwhile, put the bulgur wheat in a heatproof bowl, season with salt and pour over boiling water to cover. Leave to stand for 20 minutes until tender, then drain well. Add the tomatoes, cucumber and herbs to the bulgur wheat, drizzle over the lemon juice and remaining oil, season to taste with pepper and toss to combine. Gently fold in the squash and smoked trout, check the seasoning and serve.

SALMON BROCHETTES WITH PEACH & CUCUMBER SALAD SERVES 4

320g/11oz cherry tomatoes
4 salmon fillets, cubed
1 tsp grated fresh root ginger
grated zest and juice of ½ lime
1 tbsp olive oil
salt and freshly ground black pepper

FOR THE DRESSING
2½ tsp red wine vinegar
2 tbsp olive oil
pinch of sugar
1 tsp chopped mint

FOR THE SALAD
4 peaches
320g/11oz cucumber, thinly sliced lengthways

Soak 8 bamboo skewers in water for 20 minutes. Thread the tomatoes and salmon cubes on to the skewers. Whisk together the ginger, lime zest and juice and oil and season with salt and pepper. Drizzle the mixture over the skewers, turning them to coat all over. Preheat the grill, then cook the skewers for about 10 minutes until the salmon is cooked, turning occasionally. Meanwhile, to make the dressing, whisk together the vinegar, oil, sugar and mint and season to taste with salt and pepper. To make the salad, put the peaches in a bowl, pour over boiling water to cover and leave to stand for 30 seconds. Drain, then carefully peel away the skins. Cut the flesh away from the pits in wedges, then combine with the cucumber. Drizzle with the dressing, toss well and serve with the skewers.

SMOKED MACKEREL PÂTÉ WITH PEPPER & TOMATO SALAD SERVES 4

280g/10oz smoked mackerel fillets, skinned
½–1 tsp grated horseradish
125ml/4fl oz/½ cup low-fat bio yogurt
small handful of flat-leaf parsley, chopped
freshly ground black pepper
wholemeal toast, to serve

FOR THE SALAD
2 yellow peppers, deseeded and diced
320g/11oz deseeded tomatoes, diced
handful of coriander leaves, chopped

FOR THE DRESSING
1 tbsp red wine vinegar

2½ tbsp olive oil
pinch of sugar
salt

Flake the mackerel and put it in a food processor. Add the horseradish and yogurt and a good grinding of black pepper and process to make a smooth pâté. Stir in the parsley and set aside or refrigerate until ready to serve. To make the salad, put the peppers, tomatoes and coriander in a bowl. To make the dressing, whisk together the vinegar, oil and sugar and season to taste with salt and pepper. Pour the dressing over the salad and toss well. Divide the salad between 4 plates and serve with the pâté and slices of toast.

●●●● BACON & VEGETABLE CONCHIGLIE SERVES 4

320g/11oz trimmed green beans, cut into
   3cm/1½in lengths
2 tbsp olive oil
4 bacon rashers, cut into bite-sized pieces
3 garlic cloves, crushed
320g/11oz mushrooms, sliced
320g/11oz cherry tomatoes, halved
320g/11oz/2 cups frozen peas, thawed
300g/10½oz conchiglie
salt and freshly ground black pepper
Parmesan cheese shavings, to scatter

Cook the beans in a pan of boiling water for 3–4 minutes until just tender. Drain and refresh under cold water. Heat the oil in a large frying pan and gently fry the bacon for about 1 minute, then add the garlic and fry for a further 1 minute. Add the mushrooms, sprinkle over a little salt and fry gently for 5 minutes. Add the tomatoes and cook for about 3 minutes, then add the peas and warm through for 2 minutes. Season to taste with salt and pepper. Meanwhile, cook the conchiglie in boiling salted water according to the packet instructions. Drain well and toss with the sauce. Serve immediately scattered with Parmesan shavings.

WARM PASTA SALAD WITH CHARGRILLED CHICKEN ●●●

SERVES 4

320g/11oz red onions, cut into wedges
1 tbsp olive oil
280g/10oz rigatoni
320g/11oz rocket
320g/11oz tomatoes, cut into bite-sized
 pieces
2 chargrilled chicken breasts, cut into
 bite-sized pieces
salt and freshly ground black pepper

FOR THE DRESSING
1½ tbsp balsamic vinegar
2 tbsp olive oil
1 tsp wholegrain mustard

Preheat the oven to 190°C/375°F/Gas 5. Put the onion wedges in a baking dish, drizzle with the oil, season with salt and pepper and roast in the hot oven for about 15 minutes until tender. Meanwhile, cook the rigatoni in boiling salted water according to the packet instructions. Drain well. To make the dressing, whisk together the vinegar, oil and mustard. Toss together the hot pasta, rocket and dressing, then scatter with the onions, tomatoes and chicken. Season with black pepper, toss lightly and serve immediately.

●●●● PENNE WITH AUBERGINE, BEAN & TOMATO SAUCE

SERVES 4

2 tbsp olive oil

2 garlic cloves, crushed

320g/11oz aubergine, cut into 5mm/¼in
  dice

320g/11oz tomatoes, skinned and chopped

12 dried apricots, chopped

good dash of Tabasco sauce

400g/14oz can kidney beans, drained and
  rinsed

250g/9oz penne

salt

grated Cheddar cheese, to serve

Heat the oil in a large frying pan and gently fry the garlic for about 1 minute. Add the aubergine, tomatoes, apricots, Tabasco and about 6 tbsp of water. Season to taste with salt, then cover and simmer gently for 10 minutes, stirring occasionally. Add a splash more water if the sauce becomes too dry. Stir in the kidney beans and cook gently for 10 minutes, stirring occasionally. Check the seasoning, adding a little more Tabasco if liked. Meanwhile, cook the penne in boiling salted water according to the packet instructions. Drain well and toss with the sauce. Serve immediately with grated Cheddar for sprinkling over.

●● SPAGHETTI WITH SPICY TOMATO & CHORIZO SAUCE

SERVES 2

2 tbsp olive oil

1 onion, finely chopped

2 garlic cloves, crushed

50g/1¾oz chorizo, chopped

2 red peppers, deseeded and diced

320g/11oz tomatoes, skinned and chopped

¼ tsp crushed dried chillies

4 tbsp white wine

280g/10oz spaghetti

salt and freshly ground black pepper

Parmesan cheese shavings, to scatter

Heat the oil in a frying pan and gently fry the onion and garlic for about 4 minutes. Add the chorizo and fry for 2–3 minutes. Add the peppers, tomatoes, chillies and wine and cook gently for about 10 minutes, stirring occasionally. Season to taste with salt and pepper. Meanwhile, cook the spaghetti in boiling salted water according to the packet instructions. Drain well and toss with the sauce. Serve immediately scattered with Parmesan shavings.

●●● FUSILLI WITH FETA & ROASTED VEGETABLES SERVES 4

320g/11oz courgettes, cut into large dice

2 red peppers, deseeded and cut into chunks

320g/11oz deseeded butternut squash, cut into large dice

1 garlic clove, cut into slivers

1 tbsp olive oil

250g/9oz fusilli

150g/5½oz feta cheese, crumbled

salt and freshly ground black pepper

1 tsp chopped mint, to scatter

Preheat the oven to 200°C/400°F/Gas 6. Put the courgettes, peppers and squash in a baking dish and scatter with the garlic. Drizzle with the oil, season with salt and pepper and toss well. Roast in the hot oven for about 25 minutes until tender, stirring once or twice. About 10 minutes before the end of the cooking time, cook the fusilli in boiling salted water according to the packet instructions. Drain well, then toss with the vegetables and stir in the feta. Season with more black pepper and serve immediately scattered with chopped mint.

PASTA WITH CREAMY SMOKED SALMON, MUSHROOM & SPINACH SAUCE SERVES 4

2 tbsp olive oil
2 garlic cloves, crushed
320g/11oz mushrooms, sliced
320g/11oz baby spinach
250ml/9fl oz/1 cup single cream
60ml/2fl oz/¼ cup white wine
115g/4oz smoked salmon, cut into strips
250g/9oz tagliatelle
salt and freshly ground black pepper

Heat the oil in a pan and gently fry the garlic for about 1 minute. Add the mushrooms to the pan and fry gently for 10 minutes. Add the spinach and sauté for 2–3 minutes until wilted, then stir in the cream and wine. Add the salmon and season to taste with salt and pepper. Meanwhile, cook the tagliatelle in boiling salted water according to the packet instructions. Drain well and toss with the sauce. Season with more black pepper and serve immediately.

ROASTED VEGETABLE COUSCOUS WITH CHICKPEAS ●●●●

SERVES 4

2 red peppers, deseeded and cut
    into chunks
320g/11oz courgettes, sliced
2 tbsp olive oil
200g/7oz/heaped 1 cup couscous
400g/14oz can chickpeas, drained
    and rinsed
320g/11oz cherry tomatoes, halved
salt and freshly ground black pepper
basil leaves, to scatter

FOR THE DRESSING
1½ tsp pesto
1½ tbsp balsamic vinegar
1½ tbsp olive oil

Preheat the oven to 200°C/400°F/Gas 6. Put the peppers and courgettes in a large baking dish, season with salt and pepper, drizzle with 1 tbsp of the oil and toss. Roast in the hot oven for about 20 minutes until tender, turning once. Put the couscous in a bowl, season with salt and pepper, and drizzle with the remaining oil. Stir with a fork, then pour over 250ml/9fl oz/1 cup boiling water and leave for 5 minutes. Whisk together the dressing ingredients. Add the chickpeas, roasted vegetables and tomatoes to the couscous, drizzle with the dressing, season with pepper and mix well. Scatter with the basil leaves and serve warm or cold.

ROCKET, FIG & ROASTED RED ONION SALAD WITH GOATS' CHEESE TOASTS SERVES 4 ●●●

320g/11oz red onions, cut into wedges
1½ tbsp olive oil
320g/11oz rocket
320g/11oz figs, cut into wedges
8 slices of baguette
150g/5½oz goats' cheese, sliced
salt and freshly ground black pepper

FOR THE DRESSING
1 tbsp balsamic vinegar
1½ tbsp olive oil

Preheat the oven to 200°C/400°F/Gas 6. Put the onions in a baking dish, drizzle with the oil, season with salt and pepper and roast in the hot oven for about 15 minutes until just tender. Arrange the rocket on 4 plates and scatter the wedges of figs on top. To make the dressing, whisk together the vinegar and oil and season to taste with salt and pepper. Preheat the grill and toast the bread slices on one side until golden, then turn them over, top with slices of goats' cheese and grill until golden and bubbling. Scatter the warm roasted onions over the salads, drizzle with the dressing, then top with the goats' cheese toasts and serve.

BEAN TORTILLA WITH TOMATO SALAD   SERVES 4

2 red peppers
2 tbsp olive oil
320g/11oz Spanish onions, thinly sliced
2 x 400g/14oz cans flageolet beans,
    drained and rinsed
3 sprigs of thyme, leaves only
6 eggs, beaten
salt and freshly ground black pepper

FOR THE SALAD
320g/11oz tomatoes
handful of basil leaves
1 tbsp balsamic vinegar
1 tbsp olive oil

Preheat the oven to 200°C/400°F/Gas 6. Put the peppers on a baking sheet and roast in the hot oven for 30 minutes. Move the peppers to a plastic bag, seal and leave for 15 minutes, then peel, deseed and slice. Heat the oil in a 23cm/9in non-stick frying pan and gently fry the onions for 25 minutes, stirring occasionally. Stir in the peppers, beans and thyme and season to taste. Season the eggs and pour over the vegetables. Jiggle the pan so that the egg slides down between the vegetables, then cook gently for about 10 minutes, pulling in the sides so all the egg gets cooked. When firm but still moist, place under a preheated grill for about 5 minutes until cooked. Meanwhile, to make the salad, slice the tomatoes and arrange on 4 plates, sprinkle with the basil, season with salt and pepper and drizzle with vinegar and oil. Serve the tortilla cut into wedges with the tomato salad.

ARTICHOKE PÂTÉ, CHERRY TOMATO & ROCKET OPEN SANDWICHES SERVES 4

320g/11oz drained, canned
   artichoke hearts
2 tbsp pesto
good pinch of crushed dried chillies
1 garlic clove, crushed
2 tbsp olive oil
4 slices of focaccia bread
320g/11oz cherry tomatoes, halved
large handful of rocket
salt and freshly ground black pepper

Put the artichoke hearts, pesto, dried chillies, garlic and oil in a food processor and blend until smooth. Season to taste with salt and pepper. Split the slices of focaccia in half horizontally and toast lightly. Spread some artichoke pâté on each focaccia toast and top with cherry tomatoes and rocket. Serve extra tomatoes on the side.

●●● BEETROOT, RED ONION & ORANGE SALAD WITH GRILLED HALLOUMI   SERVES 4

4 oranges, peel and pith removed
320g/11oz cooked beetroot, halved
   and sliced
320g/11oz red onions, halved and
   thinly sliced
1 tbsp chopped dill
250g/9oz halloumi cheese, cut into
   1cm/½in slices

FOR THE DRESSING
2½ tsp red wine vinegar
2 tbsp olive oil
1 tsp Dijon mustard

good pinch of sugar
freshly ground black pepper

Cut between the orange segment membranes to remove the flesh, reserving any juice. To make the dressing, whisk together the vinegar, oil, mustard and sugar and season with black pepper. Put the orange segments, beetroot and onion in a bowl and mix. Sprinkle over the dill, any reserved juice and the dressing. Mix well, then leave for at least 30 minutes for the flavours to mingle. Preheat the grill and grill the halloumi for about 4 minutes on each side until browned, then serve with the salad.

●● SWEETCORN FRITTERS WITH TOMATO SALSA   SERVES 4

115g/4oz/scant 1 cup plain flour, sifted
1 tsp baking powder
¼ tsp salt
¼ tsp crushed dried chillies
1 egg, beaten
150ml/5fl oz/scant ⅔ cup milk
320g/11oz/heaped 1½ cups drained,
   canned sweetcorn
oil, for greasing
salt and freshly ground black pepper

FOR THE SALSA
320g/11oz deseeded tomatoes, finely
   chopped
¼ red onion, finely diced
small handful of coriander leaves, finely
   chopped
juice of ½ lime

To make the salsa, mix the tomatoes, onion and coriander together in a bowl, squeeze over the lime juice and season to taste. Put a non-stick frying pan over a low heat. Mix the flour, baking powder, salt and chillies in a bowl and make a well in the middle. Add the egg and half the milk and gradually work in the flour to make a smooth mixture, then work in the remaining milk. Fold in the sweetcorn. Wipe the hot pan with lightly greased kitchen paper, then cook spoonfuls of the batter for about 2 minutes until golden underneath. Flip the fritters over and cook for 2 minutes more until golden. Keep them warm while you make the remaining fritters. (The batter makes about 20.) Serve warm with the salsa.

●●●● CANNELLINI BEAN & RED PEPPER DIP   SERVES 4

2 large red peppers
400g/14oz can cannelini beans, drained
   and rinsed
2 garlic cloves, crushed
1 tsp ground cumin
1 tsp ground coriander
¼ tsp ground ginger
2 tbsp olive oil
juice of 1 lime
salt and freshly ground black pepper

FOR DIPPING
320g/11oz carrots, cut into sticks
320g/11oz deseeded cucumber, cut
   into sticks
wedges of toasted pitta bread

Preheat the oven to 200°C/400°F/Gas 6. Put the peppers on a baking sheet and roast in the hot oven for about 30 minutes until blackened. Transfer the hot peppers to a plastic bag, seal and leave to cool for 15 minutes. When the peppers are cool enough to handle, peel, deseed and slice them. Put the peppers, cannellini beans, garlic, spices and oil in a food processor and blend until smooth. Squeeze in the lime juice and season to taste with salt and pepper. Spoon the dip on to 4 plates, surround with the carrot and cucumber sticks and pitta wedges and serve.

●● CIABATTAS FILLED WITH CHARGRILLED MEDITERRANEAN VEGETABLES   SERVES 2

1 courgette, cut into 5mm/¼in slices
160g/5½oz aubergine, cut into 5mm/¼in
   slices
olive oil, for brushing
2 tbsp pesto
2 tbsp mayonnaise
2 medium-sized ciabatta loaves, warmed
100g/3½oz ball of mozzarella cheese,
   sliced
salt and freshly ground black pepper

Heat a griddle pan. Brush the courgette and aubergine slices with oil and season with salt and pepper. Working in batches, cook the slices for about 3 minutes on each side until chargrilled and tender, keeping the cooked vegetables warm. In a small bowl, stir together the pesto and mayonnaise. Split the loaves in half and spread some pesto mayonnaise over the bottom half of each one. Add the chargrilled vegetables and mozzarella, season with salt and pepper and top with the other loaf halves. Serve immediately.

ROASTED PEPPER, ONION, BEAN & SALSA VERDE WRAPS SERVES 4

2 red peppers, deseeded and cut into chunks

320g/11oz red onions, cut into wedges

1½ tbsp olive oil

1 tbsp balsamic vinegar

400g/14oz can kidney beans, drained and rinsed

4 tortilla wraps

salt and freshly ground black pepper

FOR THE SALSA VERDE

2 handfuls of basil leaves

1 tbsp balsamic vinegar

½ tsp Dijon mustard

½ garlic clove, crushed

1 tbsp capers, rinsed

3 tbsp olive oil

Preheat the oven to 190°C/375°F/Gas 5. Put the peppers and onions in a baking dish, drizzle the oil and vinegar over the top and season with salt and pepper. Roast in the hot oven for about 15 minutes until tender, turning once or twice, then remove from the oven and stir in the beans. To make the salsa verde, put the basil, vinegar, mustard, garlic, capers and oil in a blender, season with pepper and blend to make a purée. Spoon a quarter of the roasted vegetables down the centre of each tortilla and drizzle some salsa over the top. Fold in one end, then roll each tortilla tightly to make a wrap and serve.

MAIN MEALS

CHICKEN BAKED WITH ONIONS, PEPPERS, TOMATOES & RED WINE SERVES 4

2 yellow peppers, deseeded and cut into
    large chunks
320g/11oz red onions, cut into wedges
2 garlic cloves, thinly sliced
2 tbsp olive oil
4 skinless, boneless chicken breasts
320g/11oz tomatoes, skinned and chopped
60ml/2fl oz/¼ cup red wine
salt and freshly ground black pepper
mashed potato or rice, to serve

Preheat the oven to 200°C/400°F/Gas 6. Put the peppers and onions in a large baking dish and scatter the garlic over the top. Season with salt and pepper, then drizzle with the oil and toss to coat. Nestle the chicken breasts in among the vegetables, then spoon the tomatoes over the top and drizzle with the wine. Bake in the hot oven for 20 minutes until the chicken is cooked through, spooning the juices over a couple of times during cooking. Serve with mashed potato or rice.

CHICKEN FAJITAS WITH AVOCADO SALSA SERVES 4

grated zest and juice of 1 unwaxed lime
1 tsp caster sugar
½ tsp dried thyme
½ tsp ground cinnamon
¼ tsp crushed dried chillies
4 skinless, boneless chicken breasts, cut
    into strips
2 tbsp sunflower oil
2 yellow peppers, deseeded and cut
    into strips
320g/11oz red onions, thinly sliced
salt

FOR THE SALSA
2 avocados, pitted and finely diced
320g/11oz deseeded tomatoes, diced

juice of 1 lime
2 red chillies, deseeded and finely chopped

TO SERVE
8 tortilla wraps, warmed
sour cream

Combine the lime zest and juice, sugar, thyme, cinnamon and chillies in a large, shallow dish. Add the chicken, season with salt and toss to coat, then cover and marinate in the fridge for at least 1 hour. Meanwhile, combine the salsa ingredients. Heat the oil in a wok, add the chicken and marinade and toss for about 1 minute. Add the peppers and onions and stir-fry for 4 minutes until the chicken is cooked and the vegetables are just tender. Serve with warm tortillas, the salsa and sour cream.

GARLIC CHICKEN WITH SPICY MANGO & CUCUMBER SALSA SERVES 4

2 garlic cloves, crushed
juice of 1 lime
1 tbsp olive oil
4 skinless, boneless chicken breasts
salt and freshly ground black pepper

FOR THE SALSA
320g/11oz pitted mangoes, diced
320g/11oz deseeded cucumber, diced
1 red chilli, deseeded and finely chopped
6 spring onions, thinly sliced
½ tsp chopped mint leaves
juice of ½–1 lime

Combine the garlic, lime juice and oil and season with salt and pepper. Pour the marinade over the chicken and turn to coat well. Cover and marinate in the fridge for at least 1 hour. Preheat the grill, then cook the chicken for 5–6 minutes on each side until cooked through. Meanwhile, to make the salsa, combine the mangoes, cucumber, chilli, spring onions and mint leaves. Season with a pinch of salt, squeeze over lime juice to taste and toss well. Serve the salsa with the chicken.

STIR-FRIED CHICKEN SERVES 4

1 tbsp mirin or sherry

1 tbsp soy sauce

2 tbsp sunflower oil

2 shallots, finely chopped

2 garlic cloves, crushed

2 tsp grated fresh root ginger

320g/11oz mushrooms, sliced

2 skinless, boneless chicken breasts,
cut into strips

320g/11oz broccoli, cut into bite-sized florets

320g/11oz sugar snap peas

320g/11oz carrots, cut into batons

handful of basil leaves, torn

freshly ground black pepper

noodles or rice, to serve

Combine the mirin or sherry and soy sauce. Heat the oil in a wok and stir-fry the shallots, garlic and ginger for about 30 seconds. Add the mushrooms and stir-fry for 1 minute, then add the chicken and stir-fry for another minute. Add the broccoli, sugar snap peas and carrots, drizzle the soy sauce mixture over and stir-fry for 2 minutes until the chicken is cooked and the vegetables are just tender but still crisp. Toss in the basil, season with black pepper and serve immediately with noodles or rice.

THAI-STYLE CHICKEN & VEGETABLE CURRY SERVES 4

2 shallots, finely chopped

2 tbsp sunflower oil

2 garlic cloves, crushed

2 tsp grated fresh root ginger

2 tsp Thai green curry paste

2 green chillies, deseeded and finely
chopped

400ml/14fl oz can coconut milk

400ml/14fl oz/1⅔ cups chicken stock

3 skinless, boneless chicken breasts, cut into
bite-sized pieces

320g/11oz carrots, cut diagonally

2 red peppers, deseeded and cut into strips

320g/11oz cabbage, shredded

juice of 1 lime

1 tsp soft brown sugar

1–2 tsp Thai fish sauce

coriander leaves, chopped, to scatter

rice, to serve

Stir-fry the shallots in the oil for 1 minute. Add the garlic, ginger, curry paste and chillies and stir-fry for a further 1 minute. Pour in the coconut milk and stock and bring to the boil. Reduce the heat and simmer gently for about 10 minutes. Add the chicken and simmer for a further 5 minutes, then add the carrots, peppers and cabbage and cook for about 3 minutes until the vegetables are just tender and the chicken is cooked through. Stir in the lime juice, sugar and fish sauce to taste, scatter with coriander leaves and serve with rice.

CREAMY CHICKEN BAKED WITH FENNEL & CARROTS

SERVES 4

4 skinless, boneless chicken breasts
1 large fennel bulb (about 320g/11oz),
   quartered and sliced
320g/11oz carrots, cut into batons
bunch of spring onions, thinly sliced
25g/1oz butter
2 garlic cloves, crushed
250ml/9fl oz/1 cup crème fraîche
125ml/4½fl oz/½ cup white wine
1 tsp Dijon mustard
salt and freshly ground black pepper
new potatoes or brown rice, to serve

Preheat the oven to 190°C/375°F/Gas 5. Put the chicken breasts in a large baking dish. Nestle the fennel and carrots around the chicken breasts and sprinkle the spring onions over the top. Melt the butter in a pan and gently fry the garlic for about 1 minute. Stir in the crème fraîche, wine and mustard and season to taste with salt and pepper. Pour the mixture over the chicken and vegetables, then bake for 20–25 minutes until the chicken is cooked through and the vegetables are tender. Serve with new potatoes or brown rice.

AUBERGINES STUFFED WITH LAMB SERVES 4

4 aubergines

2 tbsp olive oil

320g/11oz onions, finely chopped

3 garlic cloves, crushed

280g/10oz minced lamb

320g/11oz tomatoes, skinned and chopped

1 tbsp sun-dried tomato paste

1 tsp oregano leaves

60g/2¼oz/⅔ cup freshly grated Parmesan
    cheese

salt and freshly ground black pepper

4 dessert bowls of salad, to serve

Preheat the oven to 180°C/350°F/Gas 4. Halve the aubergines lengthways, scoop out the flesh (leaving the shells intact) and chop the flesh. Heat the oil in a large frying pan and gently fry the onions and garlic for about 4 minutes. Add the lamb and brown it all over. Drain off the excess fat, then add the aubergine flesh and fry gently for about 5 minutes. Add the tomatoes, tomato paste and oregano, season with salt and pepper and simmer gently for about 15 minutes, stirring occasionally. Check the seasoning. Arrange the aubergine shells in a baking dish and spoon the filling into them. Scatter the Parmesan over the top and bake for about 30 minutes until tender. Serve with side salads.

LAMB STEAKS WITH RED PEPPER RELISH & SWEETCORN COBS SERVES 4

2 garlic cloves, crushed

2 tbsp olive oil

2 red peppers, deseeded and chopped

1 tsp balsamic vinegar

handful of coriander leaves

4 sweetcorn cobs, husks and threads
    removed

4 lamb leg steaks

salt and freshly ground black pepper

To make the relish, gently fry the garlic in the oil for about 1 minute. Add the peppers and cook gently for about 20 minutes until tender. Tip into a food processor, add the vinegar and coriander, then blend briefly. Season to taste with salt and pepper. Meanwhile, cook the sweetcorn cobs in a large pan of boiling water for about 10 minutes until tender, then drain. While the corn is cooking, preheat the grill and cook the leg steaks for about 6 minutes on each side, or until cooked to your liking. Serve the lamb with the red pepper relish and sweetcorn cobs.

GRILLED LAMB CUTLETS WITH BLUEBERRY SAUCE & SAUTÉED SPINACH SERVES 4

4–8 lamb cutlets
2 tbsp olive oil
2 garlic cloves, crushed
125ml/4fl oz/1cup red wine
80ml/2½fl oz/⅓cup port
125ml/4fl oz/½ cup beef stock
320g/11oz/2 cups blueberries
2 tsp cornflour, dissolved in 2 tbsp
    cold water
320g/11oz spinach
salt and freshly ground black pepper

Preheat the grill. Season the cutlets with salt and pepper and cook for 3–4 minutes on each side until cooked to your liking. Meanwhile, to make the sauce, heat half the oil in a pan and gently fry half the garlic for about 1 minute. Add the wine, port and stock and bring to the boil, then reduce the heat slightly and simmer vigorously for 2 minutes. Add the blueberries and simmer for a further 1 minute, then add the cornflour mixture, stirring until it thickens. Season to taste with salt and pepper. While the sauce is simmering, fry the remaining garlic in the remaining oil for about 1 minute, then add the spinach and sauté for about 3 minutes until just wilted. Season to taste with salt and pepper. Serve with the lamb cutlets (1–2 per portion, as required) and blueberry sauce.

LAMB TAGINE WITH PRUNES, TOMATOES, ROASTED RED ONIONS & CHICKPEAS SERVES 4

400g/14oz lamb shoulder, trimmed and
  cubed

2 tbsp olive oil

3 garlic cloves, crushed

1 tsp ground ginger

1 tsp ground cinnamon

320g/11oz tomatoes, skinned and chopped

100g/3½oz/½ cup ready-to-eat pitted
  prunes

400g/14oz can chickpeas, rinsed and
  drained

320g/11oz red onions, cut into wedges

good squeeze of lemon juice

salt and freshly ground black pepper

couscous, to serve

In a large casserole, combine the lamb, half the oil, garlic, ginger, cinnamon and tomatoes. Season with salt and pepper, then pour 300ml/10fl oz/1¼ cups water over to cover. Bring to the boil, then reduce the heat, cover and simmer gently for about 2 hours, checking occasionally and adding a little more water if the mixture is dry. Add the prunes and chickpeas and simmer for 20 minutes more. Meanwhile, preheat the oven to 190°C/375°F/Gas 5. Put the onions in a baking dish, drizzle with the remaining oil, season and toss to coat. Roast in the hot oven for 15 minutes, then gently stir into the tagine when it is ready. Check the seasoning, add lemon juice to taste and serve with couscous.

●●● SHEPHERD'S PIE SERVES 4

3 garlic cloves, crushed

2 tbsp olive oil

450g/1lb lean minced lamb

2 red peppers, deseeded and diced

320g/11oz mushrooms, chopped

320g/11oz tomatoes, skinned and chopped

1 tbsp tomato purée

100ml/3½fl oz/scant ½ cup lamb or
    beef stock

1 tsp dried oregano

750g/1lb 10oz potatoes, cut into chunks

40g/1½oz butter

4 tbsp milk

salt and freshly ground black pepper

Preheat the oven to 220°C/425°F/Gas 7. Gently fry the garlic in the oil for about 1 minute, then add the lamb and brown it all over. Add the peppers, mushrooms, tomatoes, tomato purée, stock and oregano and bring to the boil, then reduce the heat and cook gently for about 15 minutes until the mixture is thick, stirring occasionally. Meanwhile, cook the potatoes in boiling salted water for about 10 minutes until tender, then drain and leave to steam dry. Mash the potatoes with the butter and milk until smooth and season to taste with salt and pepper. Spoon the lamb mixture into a baking dish, spoon the potatoes on top and bake for about 15 minutes until golden, then serve.

●●● LAMB BURGERS WITH AVOCADO, PEPPER & TOMATO SALSA SERVES 4

500g/1lb 2oz lean minced lamb

½ red onion, grated

1 garlic clove, crushed

1 tsp ground cumin

1 tsp paprika

2 tbsp chopped mint leaves

olive oil, for frying

salt and freshly ground black pepper

flatbreads, to serve

FOR THE SALSA

320g/11oz deseeded tomatoes, diced

2 green chillies, deseeded and finely
    chopped

2 yellow peppers, deseeded and diced

2 avocados, pitted and diced

handful of flat-leaf parsley, chopped

2 tbsp chopped mint leaves

1 tbsp olive oil

juice of 1 lime

Combine the lamb, onion, garlic, cumin, paprika and mint and season well with salt and pepper. Shape into 8 burgers and chill in the fridge for about 30 minutes. To make the salsa, combine the tomatoes, chillies, peppers, avocados, parsley and mint and drizzle with the olive oil. Season with salt and squeeze over lime juice to taste. Fry the burgers in oil for about 5 minutes on each side until just cooked through. Serve with the salsa and flatbreads.

PORK CASSEROLE WITH CHICKPEAS, TOMATOES, DRIED APRICOTS & ORANGE SERVES 4

1 onion, finely chopped

2 garlic cloves, crushed

2 tbsp olive oil

450g/1lb pork loin, trimmed and cubed

100g/3½oz chorizo, diced

2 tsp ground cumin

1 tsp ground coriander

12 dried apricots, chopped

320g/11oz tomatoes, skinned and chopped

2 yellow peppers, deseeded and cut into chunks

juice of 2 oranges

100ml/3½fl oz/scant ½ cup chicken stock

400g/14oz can chickpeas, rinsed and drained

juice of ½ lemon

salt and freshly ground black pepper

Gently fry the onion and garlic in the oil for about 5 minutes. Add the pork and chorizo, sprinkle the spices over and cook, stirring, for 1–2 minutes. Add the apricots, tomatoes, peppers, orange juice and stock, season with salt and pepper and stir to mix. Bring to a boil, then reduce the heat and simmer for about 45 minutes until the sauce becomes thick, stirring once or twice. Add the chickpeas and simmer for a further 10 minutes. Check the seasoning, then squeeze lemon juice over to taste.

SAUSAGES WITH CARROT & CELERIAC MASH & ONION GRAVY SERVES 4

320g/11oz carrots, thinly sliced
320g/11oz celeriac, diced
350g/12oz potatoes, diced
40g/1½oz butter
8–12 good-quality pork sausages
salt

FOR THE GRAVY
320g/11oz onions, sliced
3 tbsp olive oil
400ml/14fl oz/1⅔ cups vegetable
    or chicken stock
½–1 tsp soy sauce
freshly ground black pepper

To make the gravy, fry the onions in the oil for about 15 minutes until soft and golden, stirring frequently. Transfer to a blender or food processor, add the stock and blend until smooth. Return to the pan, stir in the soy sauce and pepper to taste, and keep warm. Meanwhile, put the carrots, celeriac and potatoes in a large pan with 3 tbsp water. Sprinkle with a little salt, cover and simmer gently for about 15 minutes until tender, shaking the pan frequently. Add the butter and mash the vegetables until smooth. Season to taste with salt and pepper. While the vegetables cook, preheat the grill and grill the sausages until browned and cooked through, turning several times. Serve with the mash and gravy.

MARINATED PORK CHOPS WITH ROASTED APPLES, SQUASH & RED ONIONS SERVES 4

1 tsp ground cumin
1 tsp ground cinnamon
1 tbsp soy sauce
2 tbsp honey
1 tbsp lemon juice
4 pork loin steaks
2 tbsp sunflower oil
1 tbsp balsamic vinegar
320g/11oz red onions, cut into wedges
320g/11oz deseeded squash, cut into
    chunks
320g/11oz peeled, cored apples, cut
    into chunks
salt and freshly ground black pepper

Combine the cumin, cinnamon, soy sauce, honey and lemon juice and season with black pepper. Pour the marinade over the pork steaks and turn to coat. Cover and marinate in the fridge for at least 1 hour. Preheat the oven to 200°C/400°F/Gas 6. Whisk together the oil and vinegar. Put the onions, squash and apples in a large baking dish and season well with salt and pepper. Pour the oil and vinegar mixture over the top and toss to coat. Bake in the hot oven for about 30 minutes until the vegetables and apples are tender. About 15 minutes before the end of the cooking time, preheat the grill. Put the pork steaks on the grill rack and grill for about 6 minutes on each side until just cooked through. Serve with the roasted vegetables and apples.

BACON, PEA & MUSHROOM RISOTTO   SERVES 4

3 garlic cloves, crushed

3 tbsp olive oil

320g/11oz mushrooms, sliced

4 bacon rashers, cut into bite-sized pieces

280g/10oz/1¼ cups risotto rice

180ml/6fl oz/¾ cup white wine

about 1.25 litres/2 pints/5 cups boiling
    vegetable stock

320g/11oz/2 cups frozen peas, thawed

60g/2¼oz/⅔ cup freshly grated Parmesan
    cheese, plus shavings to scatter

salt and freshly ground black pepper

Gently fry half the garlic in half the oil for 1 minute. Add the mushrooms and a sprinkling of salt and cook gently for about 10 minutes until the mushrooms are tender and the juices have evaporated. Transfer to a bowl. Heat the remaining oil in the pan and fry the bacon for about 2 minutes. Add the remaining garlic and fry for 1 minute, then add the rice and cook for 1–2 minutes. Add the wine and simmer until nearly absorbed, stirring frequently. Repeat with a ladle of boiling stock, then keep adding stock for 20 minutes until the rice is tender. (You might not need all the stock.) Stir in the mushrooms and peas and warm through, then stir in the grated Parmesan. Season to taste with salt and pepper and serve with Parmesan shavings.

THAI-STYLE GREEN PORK CURRY   SERVES 4

2 tbsp sunflower oil

3 tbsp green curry paste

1 green chilli, deseeded and finely
    chopped

600ml/21fl oz/2½ cups coconut milk

4 kaffir lime leaves, shredded

400g/14oz pork loin, thinly sliced

2 red peppers, deseeded and cut into strips

320g/11oz baby corn, halved

320g/11oz sugar snap peas

320g/11oz broccoli, cut into bite-sized florets

1 tbsp Thai fish sauce

1 tsp soft brown sugar

juice of 1 lime

coriander or basil leaves, to scatter

rice, to serve

Heat the oil in a wok. Add the curry paste and chilli and stir-fry for about 1 minute. Stir in the coconut milk and lime leaves, then add the pork and bring to the boil. Reduce the heat and simmer gently for about 2 minutes. Add the peppers, baby corn, sugar snap peas and broccoli and simmer for about 2 minutes until the pork is cooked through and the vegetables are just tender. Stir in the fish sauce, sugar and lime juice to taste. Scatter over the herbs and serve with rice.

PEPPERONI & ARTICHOKE PIZZAS SERVES 4

2 garlic cloves, crushed

2 tbsp olive oil, plus extra for brushing

320g/11oz tomatoes, skinned and chopped

handful of basil leaves

2 x 25cm/10in ready-made pizza bases

2 x 100g/3½oz balls of mozzarella cheese,
  sliced

100g/3½oz thinly sliced pepperoni

320g/11oz drained bottled or canned
  artichokes, quartered

salt and freshly ground black pepper

Preheat the oven to 220°C/425°F/Gas 7. Gently fry the garlic in the oil for about 1 minute, then add the tomatoes, season with salt and pepper and cook gently for about 15 minutes. Transfer to a food processor, add the basil and blend until smooth. Check the seasoning. Brush 2 baking sheets with oil, put the pizza bases on them and spread with the tomato sauce. Top with the mozzarella, pepperoni and artichokes and bake for 15–20 minutes until golden and bubbling. Serve cut into wedges.

BEEF CURRY WITH TOMATOES, ONIONS & SPINACH

SERVES 4

450g/1lb lean minced beef

1 tbsp sunflower oil

320g/11oz onions, chopped

3 garlic cloves, crushed

2 green chillies, deseeded and chopped

2 tsp ground cumin

1 tsp ground coriander

1 tsp ground cinnamon

½ tsp turmeric

320g/11oz tomatoes, skinned and chopped

80ml/2½fl oz/⅓ cup beef stock

320g/11oz baby spinach

naan breads, to serve

Heat a frying pan and dry fry the beef all over for about 5 minutes. Transfer to a plate using a slotted spoon. Add the oil to the pan and gently fry the onion and garlic for 4 minutes. Add the spices and fry for a further 2 minutes. Return the beef to the pan with the tomatoes and stock. Bring to the boil, cover with a lid, then simmer very gently for about 30 minutes. Stir in the spinach and cook for about 2 minutes until wilted. Serve with naan breads.

STIR-FRIED BEEF WITH MIXED VEGETABLES SERVES 4

2 tbsp sunflower oil
320g/11oz onions, sliced
320g/11oz deseeded butternut squash,
    sliced
320g/11oz sugar snap peas
4 tbsp soy sauce
4 tbsp caster sugar
1 red chilli, deseeded and chopped
2 tsp grated fresh root ginger
1 tbsp Thai fish sauce
1 tsp five spice powder
1 tbsp oyster sauce
450g/1lb fillet steak, thinly sliced
320g/11oz pak choi, halved or quartered
    if large
handful of basil leaves, torn

Heat the oil in a wok, then stir-fry the onions and squash for 2 minutes. Reduce the heat and cook gently for 3 minutes. Add the sugar snap peas and cook for 3 minutes until just tender. Meanwhile, heat the soy sauce, sugar, chilli, ginger, fish sauce, five spice powder and oyster sauce in another wok or a large frying pan, stirring, for about 3 minutes. Add the beef and cook for about 3 minutes. Add the stir-fried vegetables and the pak choi and cook for 1 minute until the pak choi is just tender. Add the basil and serve immediately.

CHILLI CON CARNE SERVES 4

320g/11oz onions, finely chopped
2 garlic cloves, crushed
2 tbsp olive oil
450g/1lb lean minced beef
2 tsp ground cumin
1/4 tsp crushed dried chillies
1 tsp paprika
320g/11oz tomatoes, skinned and chopped
1 tbsp sun-dried tomato paste
320g/11oz mushrooms, sliced
150ml/5fl oz/scant 2/3 cup beef stock
400g/14oz can kidney beans, rinsed and
    drained
salt and freshly ground black pepper
coriander leaves, to scatter

TO SERVE
rice
sour cream

Gently fry the onions and garlic in the oil for 4 minutes. Add the beef and brown it all over, then drain off as much of the fat as you can. Stir in the spices, tomatoes, tomato paste, mushrooms and stock. Season to taste with salt and pepper and bring to the boil, then reduce the heat, cover and simmer for about 10 minutes. Add the kidney beans and cook gently for a further 10–15 minutes, then check the seasoning. Scatter with coriander and serve with rice and a dollop of sour cream.

PAN-FRIED STEAKS WITH CREAMY MUSHROOM & PEPPER SAUCE SERVES 4

3 garlic cloves, crushed

2 tbsp olive oil, plus extra for brushing

320g/11oz mushrooms, sliced

2 green peppers, deseeded and sliced

180ml/6fl oz/¾ cup single cream

juice of ¼ lemon

4 x 175g/6oz rump steaks

salt and freshly ground black pepper

Gently fry the garlic in the oil for about 1 minute. Add the mushrooms and peppers, season with a little salt, and fry for about 5 minutes until tender. Add the cream and simmer briefly, then season to taste with black pepper and a good squeeze of lemon juice. Meanwhile, season the steaks with salt and pepper and brush with oil. Heat a non-stick frying pan until very hot, then cook the steaks for about 2 minutes on each side until done to your liking. Serve with the creamy mushroom and pepper sauce.

MEATBALLS WITH A RICH TOMATO & PEPPER SAUCE SERVES 4

2 red peppers, deseeded and cut into chunks

2 tbsp olive oil

350g/12oz lean minced beef

½ onion, grated

2 garlic cloves, crushed

2 tbsp freshly grated Parmesan cheese

2 tsp thyme

320g/11oz tomatoes, skinned and chopped

1 tbsp tomato purée

80ml/2½fl oz/⅓ cup beef stock

salt and freshly ground black pepper

Preheat the oven to 200°C/400°F/Gas 6. Put the peppers in a baking dish, drizzle with half the oil, season with salt and pepper and roast in the hot oven for about 20 minutes until tender. Meanwhile, put the beef, onion, garlic, Parmesan and half the thyme in a bowl. Season with salt and pepper and mix well. Roll the mixture into 35–40 bite-sized balls. Heat the remaining oil in a large, non-stick pan until hot, then add the meatballs and brown them all over, working in batches if necessary. Add the tomatoes, tomato purée, stock, peppers and remaining thyme to the pan and season with salt and pepper, then simmer gently for about 20 minutes until the meatballs are cooked.

FRIED RICE WITH BEEF & VEGETABLES SERVES 4

2 tbsp sunflower oil

2 garlic cloves, crushed

2 tsp green curry paste

200g/7oz lean beef steak, thinly sliced

320g/11oz broccoli, cut into bite-sized pieces

2 red peppers, deseeded and cut into strips

250g/9oz cooked rice

3 tbsp light soy sauce

1 tsp soft brown sugar

1 tbsp Thai fish sauce

320g/11oz/3½ cups beansprouts

handful of coriander leaves

freshly ground black pepper

Heat the oil in a wok, then stir-fry the garlic and green curry paste for about 30 seconds. Add the beef and stir-fry for about 2 minutes until it is just cooked through. Toss the broccoli, peppers, rice, soy sauce, sugar and fish sauce into the wok and stir-fry for about 2 minutes. Add the beansprouts and stir-fry for 1 minute. Season with black pepper, stir in the coriander and serve immediately.

SEAFOOD PAELLA SERVES 4

2 tbsp olive oil

1 onion, finely chopped

2 garlic cloves, crushed

80g/2¾oz chorizo, chopped

320g/11oz tomatoes, skinned and chopped

80ml/2½fl oz/⅓ cup sherry

550ml/19fl oz/2¼ cups chicken stock

pinch of saffron threads

200g/7oz/1 cup paella rice

320g/11oz courgettes, quartered and sliced

320g/11oz/2 cups frozen peas, thawed

350g/12oz cooked mixed seafood

handful of flat leaf parsley, chopped

salt and freshly ground black pepper

lemon wedges, to serve

Heat the oil in a paella pan or large frying pan and gently fry the onion and garlic for 4 minutes. Add the chorizo and fry for 3 minutes, then add the tomatoes and cook gently for 5 minutes. Stir in the sherry, stock and saffron, followed by the rice, then season well with salt and pepper and spread the mixture evenly over the pan. Bring to the boil, then reduce the heat and simmer for 10 minutes. Add the courgettes and cook for 15 minutes, stirring occasionally, then stir in the peas and seafood and cook for about 3 minutes to warm through and until the rice is tender. Cover and leave to stand for 5 minutes, then scatter with parsley and serve with lemon wedges for squeezing over.

TOMATO-BAKED TROUT WITH HERBY PUY LENTILS

SERVES 4

200g/7oz/1 cup Puy lentils
4 tbsp sherry
bunch of spring onions, thickly sliced
3 tbsp double cream
large handful of basil leaves, torn
4 trout fillets
1½ garlic cloves, finely chopped
olive oil, for drizzling
320g/11oz cherry tomatoes
salt and freshly ground black pepper
320g/11oz steamed green beans, to serve

Cook the lentils in a pan of boiling water for about 30 minutes until tender. Drain well, then return to the pan. Add the sherry and spring onions and heat gently for about 3 minutes. Stir in the cream and basil and season to taste. About 20 minutes before the end of the cooking time, preheat the oven to 220°C/425°F/Gas 7. Put the trout skin-side up in a baking dish, season, sprinkle with about half the garlic and drizzle with some oil. Cut half the tomatoes in half and leave the rest whole, then arrange them all around the trout and sprinkle with the remaining garlic. Season and drizzle with more oil. Roast for about 12 minutes or until the fish is cooked through. Serve with the lentils and green beans.

SEARED TUNA WITH AVOCADO & KIWI FRUIT SALSA

SERVES 4

4 tuna steaks
oil, for brushing
salt and freshly ground black pepper

FOR THE SALSA
2 avocados, pitted and finely diced
4 large kiwi fruit, diced
small handful of coriander, chopped
juice of ½–1 lime

To make the salsa, combine the avocados, kiwi fruit and coriander and season with salt and pepper. Squeeze the lime juice over, toss well and set aside. Brush the tuna steaks with oil and season with salt and pepper. Heat a non-stick pan until hot, add the fish and sear for 1–2 minutes on each side until cooked but still pink in the middle. Serve with the salsa.

GRILLED SALMON ON CHILLI PEA MASH WITH ROASTED SQUASH SERVES 4

320g/11oz deseeded butternut squash,
  cut into chunks
3 tbsp olive oil
¼ tsp crushed dried chillies, plus extra
  for sprinkling
4 salmon fillets
juice of ½ lemon, plus wedges to serve
½ onion, finely chopped
320g/11oz/2 cups peas
1½ tbsp sherry
2 tbsp crème fraîche
salt and freshly ground black pepper

Preheat the oven to 190°C/375°F/Gas 5. Put the squash in a baking dish, drizzle with some of the oil, season with salt and sprinkle with some dried chillies. Roast for about 25 minutes until tender. About 10 minutes before it is ready, preheat the grill. Put the salmon fillets on the grill rack, squeeze the lemon juice over and season with salt and pepper. Grill for 3–5 minutes on each side until the fish is just cooked through. Meanwhile, gently fry the onion in the remaining oil for about 4 minutes. Add the peas, dried chillies and sherry, bring to the boil, then cover and simmer for about 5 minutes until the peas are cooked through. Tip into a food processor and blend to a rough mash, then stir in the crème fraîche and season to taste with salt and pepper. Serve with the salmon and squash with lemon wedges for squeezing over.

COD BAKED IN A PAPER PARCEL SERVES 4

2 tsp grated fresh root ginger
320g/11oz leeks, cut into 8cm/3in strips
2 tbsp sunflower oil
320g/11oz courgettes, cut into batons
2 yellow peppers, deseeded and cut
    into strips
320g/11oz carrots, cut into batons
1 tsp sesame oil
crushed dried chillies
large handful of basil leaves, torn
4 skinless cod fillets (about 150g/5½oz each)
½ lemon, cut into 4 wedges
salt

Preheat the oven to 190°C/375°C/Gas 5. Cut out
4 x 35cm/14in squares of greaseproof paper. Gently
fry the ginger and leeks in the oil for 2 minutes,
then add the courgettes, peppers and carrots and
fry for 3 minutes. Stir in the sesame oil and basil leaves
and season to taste with salt and dried chillies. Divide
the vegetables among the sheets of greaseproof paper,
piling them up in the centre. Season the fish fillets and
place one on top of each pile of vegetables. Squeeze a
wedge of lemon over each portion, then bring the paper
over the top and scrunch it up to make tightly sealed
parcels. Place the parcels on a baking sheet and bake
for about 15 minutes until the fish is cooked through.

FISH PIE WITH RICH TOMATO SAUCE SERVES 4

1 onion, chopped
2 garlic cloves, crushed
2 tbsp olive oil
320g/11oz tomatoes, skinned and chopped
40g/1½oz butter
40g/1½oz plain flour
450ml/16fl oz/1¾ cups milk
good pinch of crushed dried chillies
320g/11oz carrots, sliced
320g/11oz celeriac, diced
450g/1lb potatoes, diced
60g/2¼oz butter
350g/12oz haddock or cod, skinned
350g/12oz cooked mixed seafood
salt and freshly ground black pepper
320g/11oz/2 cups boiled peas, to serve

Preheat the oven to 200°C/400°F/Gas 6. Gently fry the
onion and garlic in the oil for 4 minutes. Add the tomatoes,
season and simmer for 10 minutes. Meanwhile, to make
the white sauce, melt the butter in a pan and stir in the
flour. Remove from the heat and gradually add the milk,
stirring constantly, then return the pan to the heat and
stir until smooth and thick. Pour into the tomato mixture
with the chillies. Put the carrots, celeriac and potato in a
large pan, add 4 tbsp water, cover tightly and simmer for
15 minutes until tender, shaking the pan frequently. Add
the butter, mash well and season. Poach the fish in water
for 4 minutes, drain and flake into large chunks. Fold the
fish and seafood into the sauce and pour into a baking
dish. Spread the mash over the fish and bake for 30
minutes. Serve with peas.

CANNELONI FILLED WITH BEEF, TOMATO, CARROT & CELERY SERVES 4

3 garlic cloves, crushed

2 tbsp olive oil

320g/11oz carrots, diced

320g/11oz celery, diced

450g/1lb lean minced beef

320g/11oz tomatoes, skinned and diced

2 x recipe quantity white sauce (see
page 136, Fish Pie with Rich Tomato Sauce)

16 dried canneloni tubes

60g/2¼oz/⅔ cup freshly grated Parmesan
cheese

salt and freshly ground black pepper

Preheat the oven to 190°C/375°F/Gas 5. Gently fry the garlic in the oil for about 1 minute. Add the carrots and celery and cook for 5 minutes until tender. Add the minced beef and brown it gently for about 10 minutes, breaking up the lumps with a wooden spoon. Add the tomatoes and cook gently for 10 minutes. Season to taste with salt and pepper. Spoon a little of the white sauce into the bottom of a baking dish. Spoon the beef filling into the canneloni tubes and arrange in the baking dish in a single layer. Pour the remaining sauce over, scatter with grated Parmesan and bake for 35–40 minutes until the pasta is tender. Leave to stand for 10 minutes before serving.

CONCHIGLIE WITH SEAFOOD SAUCE SERVES 4

3 garlic cloves, crushed

2 tbsp olive oil

320g/11oz celery, diced

320g/11oz carrots, diced

320g/11oz tomatoes, skinned and chopped

4 tbsp white wine

¼ tsp crushed dried chillies

200g/7oz cooked mixed seafood

350g/12oz conchiglie

salt

Gently fry the garlic in the oil for about 4 minutes, then add the celery and carrots and fry for about 5 minutes until tender. Stir in the tomatoes, wine and chillies and seaon with salt. Bring to the boil, then simmer gently for about 5 minutes. Check the seasoning, then stir in the seafood and warm through. Meanwhile, cook the pasta in boiling salted water according to the packet instructions. Drain well, then stir into the seafood sauce and serve immediately.

MACARONI CHEESE WITH HAM, CAULIFLOWER & BROCCOLI SERVES 4

320g/11oz cauliflower, cut into bite-sized
   florets
320g/11oz broccoli, cut into bite-sized florets
60g/2¼oz butter
1 onion, finely chopped
60g/2¼oz/generous ⅓ cup plain flour
800ml/27fl oz/3⅓ cups milk
150g/5½oz mature Cheddar cheese, grated
115g/4oz ham, chopped
280g/10oz macaroni or other short pasta
50g/1¾oz/½ cup freshly grated Parmesan
   cheese
salt and freshly ground black pepper

Preheat the oven to 190°C/375°F/Gas 5. Cook the vegetables in a pan of boiling salted water for 4 minutes until just tender. Drain and refresh under cold water. Melt the butter in a pan and gently fry the onion for 4 minutes. Stir in the flour and cook for 1 minute, then gradually stir in the milk to form a thick sauce. Remove from the heat, stir in the cheese and ham and season to taste with salt and pepper. Meanwhile, cook the pasta in boiling salted water according to the packet instructions, then drain well. Stir the pasta and vegetables into the cheese sauce. Tip the mixture into a baking dish, scatter with cheese and bake for about 20 minutes until golden.

MUSHROOM, SPINACH & LENTIL LASAGNE SERVES 4

225g/8oz/1 cup Puy lentils
3 garlic cloves, crushed
2 tbsp olive oil
320g/11oz mushrooms, sliced
320g/11oz tomatoes, skinned and chopped
2 tsp sun-dried tomato paste
1 tsp dried oregano
320g/11oz spinach
175g/6oz lasagne sheets
2 x recipe quantity white sauce (see
   page 136, Fish Pie with Rich Tomato Sauce)
3–4 tbsp freshly grated Parmesan cheese
salt and freshly ground black pepper

Cook the lentils in a pan of boiling water for about 30 minutes until tender. Drain well and return to the pan. Preheat the oven to 180°C/350°F/Gas 4. Gently fry the garlic in the oil for about 1 minute. Add the mushrooms and fry for 5 minutes. Stir in the tomatoes, tomato paste, lentils and oregano, season with salt and pepper and simmer gently for about 10 minutes. Stir in the spinach and cook for 2 minutes until just wilted. Spoon half of the spinach mixture into a baking dish, top with a layer of lasagne sheets and spread slightly less than half the white sauce on top. Repeat the 3 layers and scatter the grated Parmesan over the top. Bake for about 40 minutes until golden and bubbling.

CHICKEN & SPRING VEGETABLE PASTA BAKE SERVES 4

320g/11oz trimmed asparagus, cut into
   2cm/¾in lengths
250g/9oz fusilli or other pasta shapes
2 garlic cloves, crushed
2 tbsp olive oil
400g/14oz can chopped tomatoes
125ml/4fl oz/½ cup double cream
320g/11oz/2 cups frozen peas, thawed
320g/11oz drained canned artichokes,
   quartered
2 chargrilled chicken breasts, cut into
   bite-sized pieces
60g/2¼oz/⅔ cup freshly grated
   Parmesan cheese
salt and freshly ground black pepper

Preheat the oven to 190°C/375°F/Gas 5. Bring 5cm/2in of water to the boil, add the asparagus and cook for about 2 minutes until just tender. Drain, refresh under cold water and set aside. Cook the pasta in boiling salted water according to the packet instructions, then drain well. Meanwhile, gently fry the garlic in the oil for about 1 minute. Add the tomatoes, season with salt and pepper and simmer gently for 10 minutes. Stir in the cream, vegetables, chicken and pasta, check the seasoning and warm through. Transfer to a baking dish, scatter the grated Parmesan over the top and bake in the oven for 15 minutes until golden.

PENNE WITH FRESH TOMATO, ANCHOVY & CAPER SAUCE SERVES 4

3 garlic cloves, crushed
1 small onion, finely chopped
2 tbsp olive oil
320g/11oz tomatoes, skinned and chopped
1 tbsp capers
50g/1¾oz can anchovy fillets, drained and
   chopped
320g/11oz spinach
350g/12oz penne
salt and freshly ground black pepper
Parmesan cheese shavings, to scatter

Gently fry the garlic and onion in the oil for about 4 minutes. Add the tomatoes and cook gently for about 10 minutes, stirring occasionally. Stir in the capers, anchovies and spinach and cook gently for about 2 minutes until the spinach has wilted. Season with black pepper. Meanwhile, cook the pasta in boiling salted water according to the packet instructions. Drain well, mix with the sauce and serve immediately scattered with Parmesan shavings.

ROASTED RED ONION & BRIE TARTS WITH TOMATO COULIS SERVES 4

260g/9½oz ready-rolled puff pastry
175g/6oz Brie, sliced
2½ tsp sweet chilli sauce
320g/11oz red onions, cut into wedges
2 tbsp olive oil, plus extra for drizzling
2 garlic cloves, crushed
320g/11oz tomatoes, skinned and chopped
handful of basil leaves
salt and freshly ground black pepper

Preheat the oven to 220°C/425°F/Gas 7. Cut the pastry into 4 x 12cm/5in squares and put on a baking sheet. Score a line all around each square about 1cm/½in inside the edge of the pastry. Top the pastry squares with the Brie slices, arranging them just inside the scored border. Drizzle the cheese with sweet chilli sauce and top with the onion wedges. Sprinkle the onions with salt and pepper and drizzle with oil, then bake the tarts for 15–20 minutes until the onions are tender and the pastry crisp and golden. Meanwhile, gently fry the garlic in the oil for about 1 minute, then add the tomatoes, season with salt and pepper and cook gently for about 15 minutes. Transfer to a food processor or blender, add the basil and blend until smooth. Check the seasoning and serve with the tarts.

VEGETABLE BAKE TOPPED WITH CRISPY BREADCRUMBS & CHEESE SERVES 4

1 onion, finely chopped

2 garlic cloves, crushed

2 tbsp olive oil

320g/11oz button mushrooms, halved

320g/11oz carrots, diced

2 green peppers, deseeded and diced

1 recipe quantity white sauce (see
    page 136, Fish Pie with Rich Tomato Sauce)

½ tsp dried thyme

400g/14oz can Puy or green lentils, drained
    and rinsed

115g/4oz/2 cups fresh breadcrumbs

150g/5½oz Cheddar cheese, grated

salt and freshly ground black pepper

Preheat the oven to 190°C/375°F/Gas 5. Gently fry the onion and garlic in the oil for 4 minutes. Add the mushrooms, sprinkle over a little salt and fry for about 10 minutes until the juices have evaporated. Add the carrots and peppers and cook for about 5 minutes, then stir in the white sauce, thyme and lentils and heat through. Season to taste with salt and pepper, then turn into a baking dish. Mix together the breadcrumbs and grated cheese, scatter them over the top of the vegetables and press down gently. Bake for about 20 minutes until crisp and golden, then serve.

AUBERGINE, CHEESE & TOMATO STACKS SERVES 4

2 garlic cloves, crushed

2 tbsp olive oil, plus extra for brushing

320g/11oz tomatoes, skinned and chopped

handful of basil leaves, torn, plus extra
    leaves to scatter

320g/11oz aubergine, cut into 12 x 1cm/½in
    thick slices

1½ x 100g/3½oz balls of mozzarella cheese,
    cut into 12 slices

4 tbsp crème fraîche

salt and freshly ground black pepper

TO SERVE

4 dessert bowls of salad

garlic bread

Gently fry the garlic in the oil for about 1 minute. Add the tomatoes, season with salt and pepper and cook gently for about 15 minutes. Stir in the basil and check the seasoning. Meanwhile, preheat the oven to 200°C/400°F/Gas 6 and heat a griddle pan. Brush the aubergine slices with oil on both sides and season. Working in batches, press the aubergines on to the griddle pan and cook for about 3 minutes on each side until charred and tender. Put the slices in a baking dish in a single layer and top each one with a slice of mozzarella, 1 tsp crème fraîche and a good dollop of tomato sauce. Bake in the hot oven for about 15 minutes until hot and sizzling, sprinkle with basil leaves and serve with side salads and garlic bread.

COURGETTE & ASPARAGUS RISOTTO SERVES 4

320g/11oz trimmed asparagus
1 onion, finely chopped
2 garlic cloves, crushed
2 tbsp olive oil
280g/10oz/1½ cups risotto rice
180ml/6fl oz/¾ cup white wine
about 1.25 litres/2 pints/5 cups boiling
    vegetable stock
320g/11oz courgettes, quartered and sliced
60g/2¼oz/⅔ cup freshly grated Parmesan
    cheese, plus shavings to scatter
2 tsp chopped dill
salt and freshly ground black pepper

Cut the tips off the asparagus spears and slice the stems. Bring 5cm/2in of water to the boil, add the asparagus tips and cook for about 2 minutes until just tender. Drain and refresh under cold water. Gently fry the onion and garlic in the oil for 4 minutes, then stir in the rice and cook for 2 minutes. Add the wine and simmer, stirring, until nearly absorbed. Repeat with a ladle of stock, then continue adding stock for 10 minutes. Add the courgettes and asparagus stems and continue cooking and adding stock in this way for a further 10 minutes until the rice is tender. (You may not need all the stock.) Stir in the grated Parmesan, asparagus tips and dill, season to taste and scatter with Parmesan shavings.

SPINACH & ROASTED RED PEPPER FRITTATA   SERVES 4

2 red peppers, deseeded and cut
   into large chunks

3 tbsp olive oil

¼ tsp crushed dried chillies

2 garlic cloves, crushed

320g/11oz spinach

6 eggs

½ tsp dried oregano

salt

4 dessert bowls of salad, to serve

Preheat the oven to 200°C/400°F/Gas 6. Put the peppers in a large baking dish and drizzle with 1 tbsp of the oil. Season with salt, sprinkle with the chillies and toss well. Roast for about 20 minutes until tender. Heat the remaining oil in a 23cm/9in frying pan with heatproof handle and gently fry the garlic for 1 minute. Add the spinach and fry for 3–4 minutes until tender and wilted. Drain any excess liquid from the pan, then stir in the peppers. Beat the eggs with the oregano and season with salt, then pour them over the vegetables, stirring briefly so that the eggs spread through them. Cook gently for about 10 minutes, pulling the edge of the frittata away from the pan as it sets and letting the uncooked egg run underneath. Preheat the grill. When the frittata is firm but still moist on top, place it under the grill and cook for about 5 minutes until set and golden. Serve hot or warm with side salads.

SQUASH STUFFED WITH BLUE CHEESE & LEEKS SERVES 4

2 small squash (about 400g/14oz each),
   halved and deseeded
320g/11oz leeks, sliced
2 tbsp olive oil
handful of walnuts
150g/5½oz blue cheese or goats' cheese,
   diced
juice of ¼ lemon
salt and freshly ground black pepper

Preheat the oven to 190°C/375°F/Gas 5. Put the squash in a baking dish and bake for about 25 minutes until the flesh is tender. Remove from the oven and increase the temperature to 200°C/400°F/Gas 6. Gently fry the leeks in the oil for about 5 minutes until tender. Scoop out the flesh from the squash, leaving enough flesh in the skins to keep them intact, and stir the flesh into the leeks. Add the walnuts and about three-quarters of the cheese and stir well. Squeeze in the lemon juice and season to taste with salt and pepper. Pack the mixture into the squash skins, scatter the remaining cheese on top and bake for about 15 minutes until golden.

COURGETTE, RED ONION & GOATS' CHEESE CAKE WITH TOMATO SAUCE SERVES 4

100g/3½oz/½ cup couscous
3½ tbsp olive oil
4 garlic cloves, crushed
320g/11oz courgettes, grated
320g/11oz red onions, thinly sliced
100g/3½oz goats' cheese, diced
2 large handfuls of basil leaves, torn
4 eggs, beaten
320g/11oz tomatoes, skinned and chopped
salt and black pepper

Preheat the oven to 190°C/375°F/Gas 5. Put the couscous in a bowl, season with salt and rub in ½ tbsp of the oil. Pour 125ml/4fl oz/½ cup boiling water over, leave for 5 minutes, then stir with a fork. Heat 2 tbsp of the oil in a 23cm/9in ovenproof non-stick frying pan and gently fry 2 of the garlic cloves for 1 minute. Add the courgettes and cook gently for 5 minutes. Season and stir in the onions. Cook for 2 minutes, then stir in the couscous, cheese and half the basil. Season the eggs and pour evenly over the mixture. Pat down to make a firm cake, then bake for about 20 minutes until golden. Meanwhile, gently fry the remaining garlic in the remaining oil for 1 minute, then add the tomatoes. Bring to the boil and simmer for about 10 minutes. Blend with the remaining basil in a food processor until smooth, then season to taste. Serve wedges of the cake with the tomato sauce.

STIR-FRIED TOFU & VEGETABLES SERVES 4

2 tbsp sunflower oil

2 garlic cloves, crushed

2 tsp grated fresh root ginger

2 red chillies, deseeded and chopped

2 red peppers, deseeded and sliced

320g/11oz carrots, sliced

320g/11oz button mushrooms

320g/11oz cabbage, shredded

2 tbsp mirin or sherry

1–1½ tbsp soy sauce

200g/7oz deep-fried tofu, cut into cubes

handful of basil leaves, torn if large

rice, to serve

Heat the oil in a wok and stir-fry the garlic, ginger and chillies for about 30 seconds. Toss in the peppers, carrots and mushrooms and stir-fry for about 2 minutes. Add the cabbage, drizzle the mirin or sherry and soy sauce over the top and stir-fry for about 1 minute. Add the tofu and stir-fry for 30 seconds until warmed through, then stir in the basil leaves and serve with rice.

PEPPERS STUFFED WITH SPICED VEGETABLES SERVES 4

4 red peppers, halved and deseeded

1 onion, finely chopped

2 garlic cloves, crushed

2 tbsp olive oil

320g/11oz fennel bulb, diced

320g/11oz carrots, diced

320g/11oz tomatoes, skinned and diced

2 heaped tbsp sultanas

1 tsp ground cumin

1 tsp ground coriander

½ tsp ground ginger

4 tbsp toasted pine nuts

80g/2¾oz/1 cup fresh breadcrumbs

salt and freshly ground black pepper

Preheat the oven to 200°C/400°F/Gas 6. Put the peppers in a large baking dish. Gently fry the onion and garlic in the oil for 4 minutes. Add the fennel, carrots, tomatoes, sultanas and spices and cook gently for about 6 minutes. Season to taste with salt and pepper, then stir in the pine nuts and breadcrumbs. Spoon the filling into the peppers and bake in the hot oven for about 30 minutes until the peppers are tender and the stuffing is crisp and golden.

MEDITERRANEAN VEGETABLE & CHICKPEA STEW

SERVES 4

3 garlic cloves, crushed

2 tbsp olive oil

320g/11oz tomatoes, skinned and chopped

4 tbsp white wine

320g/11oz aubergine, cut into 2cm/¾in cubes

1 tsp ground cumin

1 tsp ground coriander

320g/11oz courgettes, quartered and cut into 2cm/¾in chunks

400g/14oz can chickpeas, rinsed and drained

salt and freshly ground black pepper

chopped coriander, to scatter

flatbreads or couscous, to serve

Gently fry the garlic in the oil for 1 minute. Add the tomatoes, wine, aubergine, cumin and coriander and season with salt and pepper. Stir well, bring to the boil, then cover and simmer for 10 minutes. Stir in the courgettes and chickpeas, cover and simmer for 20–25 minutes until the vegetables are tender, stirring occasionally. Check the seasoning, scatter with coriander and serve with flatbreads or couscous.

PEPERONATA PIZZAS WITH CHARGRILLED COURGETTES SERVES 4

2 garlic cloves, chopped
2 tbsp olive oil, plus extra for brushing
2 red peppers, deseeded and cut into strips
320g/11oz tomatoes, skinned and chopped
handful of basil leaves, torn
320g/11oz courgettes, cut into 6mm/¼in
    slices
2 x 25cm/10in ready-made pizza bases
2 x 100g/3½oz balls of mozzarella cheese,
    sliced
salt and freshly ground black pepper

To make the peperonata sauce, gently fry the garlic in the oil for about 1 minute, then add the peppers and cook gently for about 5 minutes. Add the tomatoes, season with salt and pepper and simmer for about 25 minutes until thick, stirring occasionally. Remove from the heat, stir in the basil and check the seasoning. Meanwhile, preheat the oven to 220°C/425°F/Gas 7 and preheat a griddle pan. Brush the courgette slices on both sides with oil and season with salt and pepper, then, working in batches, press them down on to the griddle and cook for about 3 minutes on each side until charred and tender. Spread the sauce on top of the pizza bases and arrange the courgettes and mozzarella on top. Bake for 15–20 minutes until the cheese is bubbling and the crust is golden.

LENTIL & COCONUT MILK CURRY SERVES 4

3 garlic cloves, crushed
320g/11oz onion, finely chopped
2 tbsp sunflower oil
½ tsp turmeric
½ tsp ground ginger
2 tsp ground cumin
3 red chillies, deseeded and chopped
280g/10oz/heaped 1 cup red lentils
400ml/14fl oz/1⅔ cups coconut milk
320g/11oz carrots, grated
juice of 1 lemon
salt and freshly ground black pepper
chopped coriander, to scatter
rice or naan breads, to serve

Gently fry the garlic and onion in the oil for 4 minutes, then stir in the spices and chillies. Add the lentils, coconut milk, carrots and 600ml/21fl oz/2½ cups water. Bring to the boil, then simmer gently for about 30 minutes until the lentils are tender, stirring occasionally and more frequently toward the end of the cooking time, and adding a splash more water if needed. Season with salt and pepper and squeeze in lemon juice to taste. Scatter with coriander and serve with rice or naan breads.

VEGETARIAN SAUSAGES & CHICKPEA MASH WITH SPICY TOMATO SAUCE SERVES 4

3 garlic cloves, crushed

4–5 tbsp olive oil

400g/14oz can chopped tomatoes

3 tbsp white wine

¼ tsp crushed dried chillies

1 onion, finely chopped

2 x 400g/14oz cans chickpeas, rinsed
  and drained

8–12 vegetarian sausages

salt and freshly ground black pepper

Gently fry the garlic in 1 tbsp of the oil for 1 minute. Add the tomatoes, wine and chillies, season with a little salt and simmer gently for about 25 minutes. Check the seasoning and keep the sauce warm. Gently fry the onion in 3 tbsp of the oil for 5 minutes, then add the chickpeas and 3 tbsp water, cover and warm through for 5 minutes. Remove from the heat and mash well, then stir in the remaining oil and season to taste with salt and pepper. Meanwhile, grill the sausages according to the packet instructions. Serve 2 or 3 sausages per person on a bed of mashed chickpeas with some of the spicy tomato sauce.

VEGETABLE STEW WITH DUMPLINGS SERVES 4

320g/11oz onions, halved and sliced

2 garlic cloves, crushed

2 tbsp olive oil

2 x 400g/14oz cans mixed beans, rinsed
  and drained

320g/11oz carrots, thickly sliced

320g/11oz tomatoes, skinned and chopped

½ tsp dried oregano

150ml/5fl oz/scant ⅔ cup vegetable stock

60ml/2fl oz/¼ cup cider

salt and freshly ground black pepper

FOR THE DUMPLINGS

175g/6oz/scant 1½ cups self-raising flour

pinch of salt

50g/1¾oz butter, chilled and diced

50g/1¾oz mature Cheddar cheese, grated

1 tsp chopped rosemary

To make the dumplings, put the flour and salt in a food processor, add the butter and pulse until the mixture resembles fine breadcrumbs. Stir in the Cheddar and rosemary, then work in about 100ml/3½fl oz/scant ½ cup cold water to make a soft but not sticky dough. Divide into 12 pieces and roll into balls. Gently fry the onions and garlic in the oil for 10 minutes until very soft. Add the remaining ingredients and season with salt and pepper. Bring to the boil, then reduce the heat and arrange the dumplings on top. Cover and simmer for about 20 minutes until the dumplings are risen and fluffy.

BAKED MUSHROOMS FILLED WITH SPINACH & DOLCELATTE SERVES 4

4 large, flat mushrooms, stems removed
2 shallots, finely chopped
2 tbsp olive oil
320g/11oz spinach
80g/2¾oz Dolcelatte or other creamy
   blue cheese, diced
60g/2¼oz/¾ cup fresh breadcrumbs
freshly ground black pepper

Preheat the oven to 190°C/375°F/Gas 5. Put the mushrooms in a baking dish, gill-side up. Gently fry the shallots in the oil for 2–3 minutes, then add the spinach and toss for 2–3 minutes until just wilted. Stir in the Dolcelatte until melting, then remove from the heat, stir in the breadcrumbs and season with black pepper. Spoon the spinach mixture on to the mushroom caps, then bake for 20–25 minutes until the mushrooms are tender and the filling is golden.

DESSERTS

●● MIXED-BERRY ETON MESS SERVES 4

250ml/9fl oz/1 cup double cream, whipped
125ml/4fl oz/½ cup low-fat bio yogurt
320g/11oz/2½ cups raspberries
320g/11oz/heaped 2 cups strawberries,
    hulled and cut into bite-sized pieces
    if large
8 meringue nests

Fold together the whipped cream and yogurt. Gently crush (but do not mash) the raspberries, then add them to the cream with the strawberries. Break the meringue nests into bite-sized pieces, then fold them into the cream and berry mixture. Spoon into 4 bowls and serve immediately.

FRUIT-FILLED MELONS SERVES 4

●●●●

320g/11oz/2½ cups raspberries
1½ tbsp icing sugar
320g/11oz pitted mango cut into
 bite-sized chunks
320g/11oz/2 cups blueberries
2 cantaloupe melons, halved and
 seeds removed

Put the raspberries in a blender or food processor and process until smooth. Tip the purée into a fine-mesh sieve set over a bowl and push it through with a wooden spoon to remove the pips. Stir the sugar into the purée. Combine the mango flesh with the blueberries. Put a melon half on each plate and pile the mango mixture in and around the melons. Drizzle the raspberry sauce over the top and serve.

PANNA COTTAS WITH SUMMER BERRIES & RICH FRUIT COULIS SERVES 4

●●●

3 gelatine leaves
5 tbsp milk
720ml/1¼ pints/scant 3 cups single cream
3 tbsp caster sugar
1 tsp vanilla extract
320g/11oz/2½ cups raspberries
320g/11oz/heaped 2 cups strawberries,
 hulled and cut into pieces if large
1 tbsp cassis
320g/11oz/2 cups blueberries

Soak the gelatine in the milk until soft. Put the cream and sugar in a pan and heat gently until almost boiling. Remove from the heat and allow to cool, then stir in the vanilla extract and the gelatine and milk mixture until completely dissolved. Pour the mixture into 4 x 180ml/ 6fl oz/¾ cup dariole moulds. Cover and chill overnight. To make the coulis, put about a third of the raspberries and half the strawberries in a food processor and blend until smooth. Tip the purée into a fine-mesh sieve set over a bowl and push it through with a wooden spoon to remove the pips, then stir in the cassis. To unmould the panna cottas, fill a bowl with boiling water and dip each mould into the water for 1–2 seconds. Turn each one out on to a plate and surround with the remaining berries. Drizzle the coulis over the top and serve.

●●● SUMMER PUDDING SERVES 4

320g/11oz/heaped 2 cups strawberries,
  hulled and cut into bite-sized pieces
320g/11oz/1½ cups pitted cherries
320g/11oz/2½ cups raspberries
about 150g/5½oz/⅔ cup caster sugar
8 slices of white bread, crusts removed
pouring cream, to serve

Put the fruit in a pan with 3 tbsp cold water and sprinkle over the sugar. Heat gently for about 5 minutes until the juices are released, stirring once or twice. Remove from the heat, check the sweetness, adding a little more sugar if necessary, and leave to cool. Reserving 1–2 slices of bread for the top, cut the rest into pieces and use to line the base and sides of a 1 litre/1¾ pint/4 cup pudding basin. Using a slotted spoon, transfer the fruit to the bread-lined bowl, reserving any leftover juice. Cover the pudding with the reserved slices of bread, trimming off any excess, and put a plate on top with a weight on top of that. Place in the fridge overnight, along with the reserved juices. To serve, remove the weight and plate and run a knife around the edge of the basin. Carefully invert the pudding on to a serving plate. Pour the reserved juices over the top, cut into wedges and serve with cream.

CHERRY-BERRY CRÊPES WITH WHITE CHOCOLATE SAUCE SERVES 4

320g/11oz/1½ cups pitted cherries
320g/11oz/2 cups blueberries
2 tbsp orange juice
8 ready-made crêpes

FOR THE SAUCE
100g/3½oz white chocolate, broken into
    pieces
100ml/3½fl oz/scant ½ cup double cream
1 tbsp Grand Marnier (optional)

To make the sauce, put the chocolate, cream and Grand Marnier, if using, in a small pan and heat gently, stirring until melted and combined. Keep the sauce warm. Put the cherries, blueberries and orange juice in a separate pan and heat gently for about 5 minutes until the berries are tender and juicy. Warm the crêpes according to the packet instructions, then fold each one into quarters to make a cone. Put 2 crêpes on each plate and fill each one with the fruit mixture. Drizzle with the juices and chocolate sauce and serve immediately.

●●● OVEN-POACHED PEARS & FIGS   SERVES 4

300ml/10fl oz/1¼ cups orange juice
125ml/4fl oz/½ cup port
2 tbsp caster sugar
4 cored pears
320g/11oz figs, halved
12 dried apricots
1 cinnamon stick
whipped double cream, to serve

Preheat the oven to 190°C/375°F/Gas 5. Put the orange juice, port and sugar in a small pan and stir over a gentle heat until the sugar has dissolved. Put the fruit in a baking dish, pour the orange juice mixture over the top and add the cinnamon stick. Bake in the hot oven for 25 minutes until the fruit is tender, carefully turning the fruit a couple of times during cooking. Transfer the fruit to a serving dish, using a slotted spoon. Pour the juices into a pan and boil vigorously for a few minutes until reduced and syrupy. Discard the cinnamon stick. Pour the syrup over the fruit and serve hot or cold with thick cream.

●●●● BAKED APPLES WITH PLUM & ORANGE SAUCE   SERVES 4

4 apples, cored
60g/2¼oz butter
2 tbsp soft brown sugar
1 tsp ground cinnamon
85g/3oz ready-to-eat dried figs, chopped
320g/11oz pitted plums, roughly chopped
600ml/21fl oz/2⅔ cups orange juice
1½–2 tbsp caster sugar
2 tsp cornflour, dissolved in 1 tbsp
   cold water

Preheat the oven to 180°C/350°F/Gas 4. Run a knife around the centre of each apple to cut the skin and put them in a baking dish. Put the butter, brown sugar and cinnamon in a bowl and beat until creamy, then stir in the figs. Stuff the mixture into the apple holes. Bake in the hot oven for about 30 minutes until tender. Meanwhile, put the plums in a pan with the orange juice and bring to the boil. Reduce the heat and simmer, uncovered, for about 15 minutes until the plums are tender. Pour the mixture into a blender or food processor and blend until smooth. Return to the pan and stir in caster sugar to taste. Stir in the cornflour mixture and warm through, stirring until thickened. Serve the apples and any juices spooned over the top with the plum and orange sauce.

●●●● EXOTIC FRUIT SALAD SERVES 4

320g/11oz pitted mango, sliced
320g/11oz deseeded papaya, sliced
320g/11oz cored pineapple, halved
    and sliced
320g/11oz star fruit, sliced
icing sugar, for dusting
juice of 1 lime

Divide the mango, papaya, pineapple and star fruit
between 4 bowls and dust with icing sugar. Squeeze over
the lime juice and serve.

●● BAKED BANANAS WITH MANGO SAUCE SERVES 4

4 bananas, unpeeled
320g/11oz pitted mango, roughly chopped
juice of ½–1 lime
vanilla ice cream, to serve

Preheat the oven to 180°C/350°F/Gas 4. Put the unpeeled
bananas in an ovenproof dish and bake in the hot oven for
about 20 minutes until the skins are dark and the bananas
feel soft when gently squeezed. Meanwhile, put the mango
flesh in a blender or food processor and blend to make a
purée. Stir in lime juice to taste. (The sauce should be quite
sharp.) To serve, slice the bananas open and serve with
the mango sauce and scoops of ice cream.

SUMMER BERRY SEMI-FREDDO   SERVES 4

320g/11oz/2½ cups frozen blackberries
320g/11oz/2 cups frozen blackcurrants
320g/11oz/2½ cups frozen raspberries
320g/11oz/heaped 2 cups frozen
   strawberries
100g/3½oz/heaped ⅓ cup caster sugar
250ml/9fl oz/1 cup Greek yogurt

Put about half the frozen berries in a bowl, sprinkle over half the sugar and leave to thaw at room temperature. Put the remaining berries into a food processor or blender with the yogurt and remaining sugar and blend until smooth and creamy. Check the sweetness, adding a little more sugar if needed. Scoop the mixture into 4 bowls, spoon the thawed berries over the top and serve immediately.

PEAR & PLUM SORBET SERVES 4 ●●

320g/11oz cored pears, sliced
320g/11oz pitted plums, roughly chopped
60g/2¼oz/¼ cup caster sugar
1 egg white

Put the fruit, sugar and 60ml/2fl oz/¼ cup water in a pan. Bring to the boil, then reduce the heat, cover and simmer for 10–15 minutes until tender. Transfer to a food processor and blend until smooth, then strain through a sieve set over a bowl and leave until completely cold. Stir in 80ml/6fl oz/¾ cup water and churn in an ice cream maker until thick. (Alternatively, pour the mixture into a freezer-proof container and freeze for about 4 hours until firm, whisking with a fork 2 or 3 times during freezing to break up the ice crystals or processing twice in a food processor until smooth.) Lightly whisk the egg white with a fork until just frothy, then stir into the sorbet and continue to churn, or freeze until firm enough to scoop. Put scoops of the sorbet into 4 bowls and serve immediately.

BANANA, RUM & RAISIN ICE CREAM SERVES 4 ●●

80g/2¾oz/⅔ cup raisins, roughly chopped
2 tbsp rum
250ml/9fl oz/1 cup single cream
3 egg yolks
100g/3½oz caster sugar
few drops of vanilla extract
4 ripe bananas
125ml/4fl oz/½ cup double cream

Put the raisins in a bowl, pour over the rum and leave to soak for at least 1½ hours. Meanwhile, to make the egg custard, heat the single cream in a heavy-based saucepan. Whisk the egg yolks and sugar together in a bowl until thick and pale. When the cream is almost boiling, slowly whisk it into the egg mixture and add the vanilla extract, then tip the mixture back into the pan and heat gently, stirring constantly, until bubbling. Remove from the heat and leave to cool. Mash the bananas, then stir in the rum-soaked raisins and any remaining soaking liquid, the custard and double cream. Pour the mixture into an ice cream maker and churn until thick, then turn into a freezer-proof container and freeze until firm. (If you do not have an ice cream maker, pour the mixture into a freezer-proof container and freeze for about 4 hours until firm, whisking with a fork 2 or 3 times during freezing to break up the ice crystals or processing twice in a food processor until smooth.) Scoop the ice cream into 4 bowls and serve.

●●● STRAWBERRY & BLACKCURRANT RIPPLE ICE CREAM WITH BLUEBERRIES SERVES 4

320g/11oz/2 cups blackcurrants
115g/4oz/½ cup caster sugar
320g/11oz/heaped 2 cups strawberries,
   hulled
1 recipe quantity egg custard (see page
   167, Banana, Rum & Raisin Ice Cream)
125ml/4fl oz/½ cup double cream
320g/11oz/2 cups blueberries

Put the blackcurrants in a bowl, sprinkle with the sugar and leave to stand for 30 minutes, then blend to a purée in a food processor. Tip the purée into a fine-mesh sieve set over a bowl and push it through with a wooden spoon. Check the sweetness, then refrigerate. Blend and strain the strawberries in the same way. Stir the egg custard and cream into the strawberry purée, then churn in an ice cream maker until thick. (Alternatively, pour the mixture into a freezer-proof container and freeze for about 4 hours until firm, whisking with a fork 2 or 3 times during freezing to break up the ice crystals or processing twice in a food processor until smooth.) Spoon half the ice cream into a freezer-proof container and drizzle with half the sauce, then repeat. Run a knife through the ice cream to create a marbled effect. Freeze until firm enough to scoop. Serve with the blueberries.

PEACH MELBA WITH RASPBERRY & ORANGE YOGURT ICE SERVES 4

●●●

320g/11oz/2½ cups raspberries

4 tbsp icing sugar

3 oranges, peel and pith removed to give
    320g/11oz flesh

180ml/6fl oz/¾ cup Greek yogurt

60ml/2fl oz/¼ cup double cream

4 ripe peaches, peeled, pitted and cut
    into wedges

Put the raspberries in a blender or food processor and blend to a purée. Tip the purée into a fine-mesh sieve set over a bowl and push it through with a wooden spoon to remove the pips. Sweeten to taste with about 3 tbsp of the icing sugar. Put the orange flesh in a blender or food processor with the remaining icing sugar and blend for 1 minute until smooth. Stir in half the raspberry sauce, then whisk in the yogurt and cream until smooth. Pour the mixture into a freezer-proof container and freeze for about 4 hours until firm, whisking with a fork 2 or 3 times during freezing to break up the ice crystals or processing twice in a food processor until smooth. Scoop the yogurt ice into 4 bowls, top with peach wedges and the remaining raspberry sauce and serve immediately.

FRUIT SALAD SUNDAE SERVES 4

●●●●

80g/2¾oz ready-to-eat dried figs, chopped

4 tbsp orange juice

2 tbsp brandy (optional)

320g/11oz/heaped 2 cups strawberries,
    hulled and halved, or quartered if large

320g/11oz pitted nectarines, cut into
    bite-sized wedges

320g/11oz/1½ cups pitted cherries

8 scoops of vanilla ice cream

Soak the figs in the orange juice and brandy, if using, for at least 2 hours. Put the strawberries in a food processor or blender and blend until smooth. Tip the purée into a fine-mesh sieve set over a bowl and push it through with a wooden spoon to remove the pips. Toss the fresh fruit with the figs and soaking juices, layer in tall glasses with the ice cream and strawberry purée and serve immediately.

●● RASPBERRY & KIWI FRUIT MILLE-FEUILLES   SERVES 4

250g/9oz puff pastry

320g/11oz/2½ cups raspberries

1½–2 tbsp icing sugar, plus extra for
  dusting

4 large kiwi fruit, halved and sliced

1 recipe quantity egg custard (see page
  167, Banana, Rum & Raisin Ice Cream)

125ml/4fl oz/½ cup double cream, whipped

Preheat the oven to 200°C/400°F/Gas 6. Roll out the pastry to a rectangle about 30 x 15cm/12 x 6in, then cut into 6 x 7.5 x 10cm/3 x 4in rectangles and place on a non-stick baking sheet. Bake in the hot oven for 10–15 minutes until golden and puffed up. Transfer to a wire rack to cool, then slice each pastry rectangle in half horizontally to make 12 rectangles. Put the raspberries in a food processor and blend to a purée. Tip the purée into a fine-mesh sieve set over a bowl and push it through with a wooden spoon, then sweeten with icing sugar. Fold together the egg custard and cream and spread half of it over 4 of the pastry pieces. Top with half the slices of kiwi fruit and drizzle with raspberry sauce, then top with another layer of pastry pieces, the remaining cream and kiwi fruit and more of the sauce. Top with the final pastry pieces, dust with sifted icing sugar and drizzle any remaining sauce around the outside. Serve immediately.

FRESH FRUIT TARTS SERVES 4

200g/7oz shortcrust pastry
60ml/2fl oz/¼ cup crème fraîche
1 tbsp lemon curd
320g/11oz/heaped 2 cups strawberries,
   hulled and quartered
320g/11oz pitted mango, diced

Preheat the oven to 190°C/375°F/Gas 5. Roll out the pastry on a lightly floured surface and use to line 4 x 10cm/4in loose-bottomed tart tins. Prick the bases and line with foil, then cover with baking beans and bake in the hot oven for about 10 minutes. Remove the foil and baking beans and bake for a further 5 minutes until crisp and golden. Leave to cool, then carefully remove the pastry cases from the tart tins and place on 4 plates. Combine the crème fraîche and lemon curd in a bowl and spoon into the bottom of the pastry cases. Top with most of the fruit and serve with any remainder scattered around the tarts.

●●● APPLE, PLUM & BLACKBERRY CRUMBLE SERVES 4

115g/4oz/scant 1 cup plain flour
6 tbsp soft brown sugar
115g/4oz butter, chilled and diced
60g/2¼oz hazelnuts or walnuts, roughly
　chopped
320g/11oz peeled, cored apples, sliced
320g/11oz pitted plums, chopped
320g/11oz/2½ cups blackberries
½ tsp ground cinnamon
custard or whipped double cream, to serve

Preheat the oven to 190°C/375°F/Gas 5. Put the flour and sugar in a food processor and pulse to combine, then add the butter and process until the mixture resembles breadcrumbs. Stir in the nuts. Toss together the fruit and cinnamon, then pile into a baking dish. Scatter the crumble mixture over the top and bake in the hot oven for about 45 minutes until golden and bubbling. Serve with custard or thick cream.

●●●● SQUIDGY BLUEBERRY CAKES WITH FRUIT SALAD

SERVES 4

115g/4oz butter, softened, plus extra for
　greasing
115g/4oz/½ cup caster sugar
2 eggs, beaten
115g/4oz/scant 1 cup self-raising flour
½ tsp ground cinnamon
320g/11oz/2 cups blueberries
3 oranges, peel and pith removed to give
　320g/11oz flesh, sliced
320g/11oz/1½ cups pitted cherries, halved
80g/2¾oz/½ cup pitted dates, chopped

Preheat the oven to 180°C/350°F/Gas 4. Grease 4 ramekins and line each base with greaseproof paper. Put the butter and sugar in a bowl and beat until pale and creamy, then gradually beat in the eggs. Sift the flour and cinnamon on to the mixture and fold in. Spread 2 spoonfuls of cake mixture into the bottom of each ramekin, then sprinkle a quarter of the blueberries between them. Cover with the remaining mixture and sprinkle another quarter of the blueberries on top. Bake in the hot oven for about 30 minutes until the cakes are risen and golden and a skewer inserted in the centre comes out clean. Leave to cool for a few moments, then carefully run a knife around the inside of each ramekin, turn the cakes out and leave to cool on a wire rack. Combine the oranges, cherries, dates and remaining blueberries and serve with the cakes.

●●● CITRUS PEAR & APRICOT BREAD PUDDING SERVES 4

3 oranges, peel and pith removed to give
320g/11oz flesh

200ml/7fl oz/heaped ¾ cup crème fraîche

2 tbsp caster sugar

good pinch of ground cinnamon

4 egg yolks

butter, for greasing

6 slices of white bread, crusts removed
(about 165g/5½oz)

320g/11oz cored pears, sliced

12 ready-to-eat dried apricots, chopped

Put the orange flesh in a food processor or blender and blend for about 1 minute until smooth. Put the crème fraîche, sugar, cinnamon and egg yolks in a bowl and beat until combined, then stir in the orange purée. Butter an ovenproof dish. Cut the slices of bread into quarters and arrange in the dish, scattering pear slices and apricots between each layer. Pour the orange custard over the top and leave to soak for about 15 minutes. Meanwhile, preheat the oven to 180°C/350°F/Gas 4. Bake in the hot oven for 45–50 minutes until the pudding is golden and the custard lightly set.

FRUIT SALAD WITH PUFF PASTRY PALMIERS SERVES 4

●●●●

150g/5½oz puff pastry

15g/½oz butter, melted

1 tbsp caster sugar

320g/11oz/heaped 2 cups strawberries, hulled

320g/11oz peeled, pitted nectarines, cut into thin wedges

320g/11oz cored pears, cut into thin wedges

320g/11oz/1⅔cups seedless grapes, halved

Preheat the oven to 220°C/425°F/Gas 7. Roll out the pastry on a lightly floured surface to a rectangle about 23 x 13cm/9 x 5in and trim off any rough edges. Brush the pastry with melted butter, then sprinkle with the sugar and drizzle with any remaining butter. Roll up one long side toward the centre, then roll up the other side so they meet in the middle. Slice into 8 x 1.5cm/½in thick slices and put on a non-stick baking sheet. Bake in the hot oven for 10–12 minutes until risen and golden, then transfer to a wire rack to cool. Put the strawberries in a food processor or blender and blend to make a purée. Divide the remaining fruit between 4 bowls, drizzle with the purée and serve with the palmiers.

PINEAPPLE CAKES WITH MANGO SAUCE SERVES 4

●●

60g/2¼oz butter, softened

60g/2¼oz/¼ cup caster sugar

1 egg, beaten

60g/2¼oz/½ cup self-raising flour

2 pieces stem ginger in syrup, drained and chopped

6 x 1cm/½in slices of canned pineapple, drained and chopped

320g/11oz pitted mango, roughly chopped

juice of ½–1 lime

thick cream, to serve

Preheat the oven to 180°C/350°F/Gas 4. Grease 4 x 150ml/5fl oz/scant ⅔-cup dariole moulds and line the base of each one with a disk of greaseproof paper. Put the butter and sugar in a bowl and beat until pale and creamy, then gradually beat in the egg. Fold the flour, ginger and pineapple into the mixture, then spoon into the dariole moulds, smoothing the surface. Bake in the hot oven for about 25 minutes until risen and golden and a skewer inserted in the centre comes out clean. Meanwhile, put the mango flesh in a food processor and blend to make a purée. Stir in lime juice to taste and set aside. Let the cakes cool for a couple of minutes, then run a knife around the inside of each mould and turn out on to 4 plates. Spoon the mango sauce over and around the cakes and serve with thick cream.

●●●● MIXED FRUIT PIE SERVES 4

320g/11oz cored pears, sliced
320g/11oz peeled, cored apples, sliced
320g/11oz/2 cups blueberries
12 dried apricots, chopped
2 tsp ground cinnamon
2 tbsp soft brown sugar
320g/11oz shortcrust pastry
custard or cream, to serve

Preheat the oven to 190°C/375°F/Gas 5. Combine the pears, apples, blueberries, apricots, cinnamon and sugar in a large bowl, then transfer to a deep 23cm/9in round baking or pie dish. Roll out the pastry on a lightly floured surface and cover the pie, sealing the edges and trimming off any excess. Cut 3 slits in the top of the pastry, then bake in the hot oven for about 50 minutes until the pastry is golden. Remove from the oven and leave to stand for about 15 minutes before serving with custard or cream.

UPSIDE-DOWN CRANBERRY, APPLE & CHERRY TART ●●●

SERVES 6

250g/9oz ready-rolled puff pastry
80g/2¾oz butter
115g/4oz/½ cup caster sugar
480g/1lb 1oz peeled, cored apples,
 thickly sliced
480g/1lb 1oz/4⅓ cups cranberries
120g/4½oz/generous ¾ cup dried cherries
whipped double cream, to serve

Cut out the pastry to fit over a 23cm/9in tarte tatin tin, then roll up, wrap in cling film and place in the fridge. Preheat the oven to 200°C/400°F/Gas 6. Melt the butter in the tarte tatin tin, then sprinkle over 85g/3oz/⅓ cup of the sugar. Leave to bubble for 1–2 minutes, then remove from the heat. Arrange the apples on top in a neat pattern, then return to the heat and cook for about 10 minutes until the liquid thickens and turns golden. Remove from the heat, scatter the cranberries and dried cherries over the apples and sprinkle with the remaining sugar. Press the pastry on top and bake in the hot oven for 25–30 minutes until the pastry is risen and golden. Leave to cool slightly, then carefully invert on to a serving plate. Serve hot, warm or at room temperature with thick cream.

HEALTH-BOOSTING MENUS

When you're looking to give your body a boost where it needs it most, why not try out some of these targeted menu ideas. While balance and variety is the key phrase in any healthy diet, these everyday menu selections can help you on your way to choosing the right superfood recipes for you.

BRAIN BUZZERS

Lecithin found in eggs is needed for normal brain function, while vitamin E found in avocado may reduce the effects of Alzheimer's and dementia. Oily fish such as salmon may reduce the risk of age-related dementia. Antioxidants found in blueberries are also thought to help protect the brain, so eat a handful as a snack.

BREAKFAST: Scrambled Eggs with Tomatoes & Peppers (see page 60)

LUNCH: Toasted Avocado BLT (see page 84)

DINNER: Grilled Salmon on Chilli Pea Mash with Roasted Squash (see page 135)

BONES AND TEETH

Calcium is essential for healthy bones and teeth and can be found in rich supply in milk, yogurt and cheese. Other important nutrients include magnesium found in leafy green vegetables, and manganese found in beetroot. Vitamin D, which can be found in eggs, is needed to help the body absorb calcium.

BREAKFAST: Creamy Banana, Nectarine & Strawberry Smoothie (see page 43)

LUNCH: Beetroot, Red Onion & Orange Salad with Grilled Halloumi (see page 106)

DINNER: Spinach & Roasted Red Pepper Frittata (see page 147)

EVERYDAY DETOX

We all indulge every so often, so it's good to give our body a break now and again. Try cutting out the refined carbs for a day, drink plenty of water and pack in lots of fruit, veg and lots of easy-to-digest unprocessed foods. Grapes and melons are known as natural cleansers, so these make a great choice for a snack or dessert.

BREAKFAST: Tropical Fruit Salad (see page 53)

LUNCH: Italian Bean & Cabbage Soup (see page 67)

DINNER: Cod Baked in a Paper Parcel (see page 136)

IMMUNE BOOST

Your immune system works non-stop to protect your body against illness so it's key to your good health. Vitamin C, beta-carotene, zinc and vitamin B6 are all nutrients that help to boost your immune system, so try to make sure you eat plenty of foods containing these nutrients. In this menu, you can find vitamin C in kiwi fruit, pineapple, citrus and tomatoes; beta-carotene in orange juice and squash; zinc in red meat; and vitamin B6 in squash.

BREAKFAST: Tropical Fruit Smoothie (see page 42)

LUNCH: Tabbouleh with Smoked Trout & Roasted Squash (see page 94)

DINNER: Grilled Lamb Cutlets with Blueberry Sauce & Sautéed Spinach (see page 118)

ANTI-AGERS

We're all growing older – from the day we're born. But there are lots of nutrients found in everyday foods that can help us age more gently and avoid the illnesses and diseases so commonly associated with ageing. Antioxidants, found in many fruits and vegetables, help to fight the damaging effect of free radicals that are associated with the ageing process. Potent phytochemicals found in blueberries and cherries are believed to help protect against diseases associated with ageing, while vitamin E found in kiwi can help against cancer, heart disease and Alzheimer's. Beta-carotene found in carrots and tomatoes are believed to help against macular degeneration, and lycopene found in tomatoes is believed to help against various cancers.

BREAKFAST: Summer Fruit Smoothie (see page 45)

LUNCH: Creamy Carrot, Leek & Tomato Soup (see page 68)

DINNER: Seared Tuna with Avocado & Kiwi Fruit Salsa (see page 135)

BRIGHT EYES

Several nutrients are associated with eye health and this menu tries to make the most of them. Anthocyanidins found in blueberries, strawberries and raspberries are thought to help protect against cataracts and glaucoma. Lutein and zeaxanthin found in corn and red peppers are thought to protect against cataracts and macular degeneration, and lycopene found in tomatoes has also been linked with helping against macular degeneration.

BREAKFAST: Spiced Rice Porridge with Summer Berry Compote (see page 48)

LUNCH: Simple Vegetable Minestrone (see page 68)

DINNER: Lamb Steaks with Red Pepper Relish & Sweetcorn Cobs (see page 117)

SHINY HAIR

Hair is made up almost entirely of protein so eat plenty of lamb, trout and lentils, all rich in protein, to maintain healthy locks. Other nutrients for glossy hair include omega-3 fatty acids and oils found in trout, zinc in lamb, iron in lentils, and vitamin C from raspberries, oranges, kiwis and tomatoes.

BREAKFAST: Raspberry & Orange Juice (see page 44)

LUNCH: Marinated Lamb & Kiwi Fruit Salad (see page 77)

DINNER: Tomato-baked Trout with Herby Puy Lentils (see page 134)

GOOD DIGESTION

As a general rule, the key to good digestion is plenty of fibre. Insoluble fibre can be found in almost every fruit and vegetable so this fruit- and veg-rich menu is a great starting place for a healthy, efficient digestive system. Apples are a good source of malic and tartaric acids, which helps to prevent fermentation in the digestive tract. Live (or bio) yogurt contains healthy bacteria that can be beneficial to the digestion, so why not try making the muesli with live yogurt, rather than Greek yogurt. Pineapples and papayas contain enzymes that help to aid digestion, and raspberries are believed to help cleanse the system and have traditionally been used as a natural remedy for diarrhoea and indigestion so choose one of these as a snack or dessert to follow your main meal.

BREAKFAST: Creamy Fresh Fruit Muesli (see page 46)

LUNCH: Fusilli with Feta & Roasted Vegetables (see page 100)

DINNER: Grilled Salmon on Chilli Pea Mash with Roasted Squash (see page 135)

DAIRY-FREE

Dairy foods are a great source of calcium, which is important for healthy bones and teeth. For those with a dairy intolerance or allergy, vegans, or for those who simply prefer to avoid dairy foods, it's particularly important to include plenty of other calcium-rich foods in your diet. Good sources include dark green leafy vegetables, fortified soya products, canned sardines and salmon (with bones), almonds, sesame seeds and hemp seeds. Vitamin D helps with the absorption of calcium, so get out in the sunshine and make sure you eat some oily fish regularly.

BREAKFAST: Creamy Banana, Nectarine & Strawberry Smoothie (make it with calcium-enriched soya milk – and throw a tablespoon of almonds into the blender too for an extra calcium boost) (see page 43)

LUNCH: Thai-spiced Broccoli, Spinach & Cauliflower Soup (see page 64)

DINNER: Seared Tuna with Avocado & Kiwi Fruit Salsa (see page 135)

GLUTEN-FREE

Found in wheat, barley and rye, many people are intolerant, allergic or just prefer to avoid gluten in their diet. These grains provide a useful source of energy-giving carbohydrates so it's important to choose other gluten-free, healthy carbohydrate options in their place.

BREAKFAST: Creamy Date Porridge with Baked Autumn Fruits (see page 50)

LUNCH: Rice Noodle Salad with Pork (see page 81)

DINNER: Tomato-baked Trout with Herby Puy Lentils (see page 134)

EAT A RAINBOW

It's the pigment in fruit and vegetables that gives them both their colour and health-giving properties. Enjoy fruit and veg of every colour in today's menu: yellow, orange, red, green and purple!

BREAKFAST: Raspberry & Orange Juice (see page 44)

LUNCH: Beetroot, Red Onion & Orange Salad with Grilled Halloumi (see page 106)

DINNER: Thai-style Green Pork Curry (see page 125)

ALL-DAY ENERGY

Slow-release carbohydrates found in oats and beans will help to provide you with a steady stream of energy through the day. Try serving the meatballs with wholemeal pasta as the energy is released more slowly than regular pasta. The eggs in the tortilla contain vitamin B2, which helps the body turn food into energy.

BREAKFAST: Creamy Date Porridge with Baked Autumn Fruits (see page 50)

LUNCH: Bean Tortilla with Tomato Salad (see page 104)

DINNER: Meatballs with a Rich Tomato & Pepper Sauce (see page 131)

PROTEIN POWER MENU

Muscles need protein for recovery and growth, so if you're taking lots of exercise, you need to include plenty of good-quality protein in your diet. You'll need to have plenty of carbs for energy too. The menu below is a great combination of superfoods, carbs and protein, ensuring you make the most of your keep-fit efforts.

BREAKFAST: Scrambled Eggs with Tomatoes & Peppers (see page 60)

LUNCH: Tabbouleh with Smoked Trout & Roasted Squash (see page 94)

DINNER: Grilled Lamb Cutlets with Blueberry Sauce & Sautéed Spinach (see page 118)

INDEX